GED® TEST SCIENCE

FLASH REVIEW

Related Titles

GED® Test RLA Flash Review
GED® Test Mathematical Reasoning Flash Review
GED® Test Social Studies Flash Review
GED® Test Power Practice

GED® TEST SCIENCE
FLASH REVIEW

LEARNING EXPRESS®

NEW YORK

Cataloging-in-Publication Data is on file with the Library of Congress.

Printed in the United States of America

9 8 7 6 5 4 3 2 1

First Edition

ISBN 978-1-61103-009-9

For more information on LearningExpress, other LearningExpress products, or bulk sales,
please write to us at:
    80 Broad Street
    4th Floor
    New York, NY 10004

Or visit us at:
    www.learningexpressllc.com

CONTENTS

INTRODUCTION

About the GED® Science Test

The GED® test measures how well you can apply problem solving, analytical reasoning, and critical thinking skills alongside your understanding of high-school level science. The entire test is given on a computer. On the GED® Science test, you will have 90 minutes (an hour and a half) to answer 35 questions. There are two short answer questions included, but they are not timed separately. The test will include reading passages, graphs, and charts. The majority of the information you need to answer questions will be within the exam itself, whether in a diagram or in a passage. The test does not ask you to memorize science facts beforehand.

The science topics covered on the GED® Science test are:

- **Physical science**—40% of the questions
- **Life science**—40% of the questions
- **Earth and space science**—20% of the questions

On the GED® Science test, physical science includes high-school physics and chemistry and covers the structure of atoms, the structure of matter, the properties of matter, chemical reactions, conservation of mass and energy, increase in disorder, the laws of motion, forces, and the interactions of energy and matter. Life science deals with subjects covered in high-school biology classes, including cell structure, heredity, biological evolution, behavior, and interdependence of organisms. Earth and space questions will test your knowledge of the earth and the solar system, the geochemical cycles, the origin and evolution of the earth and the universe, and energy in the earth system.

Each question on the GED® Science test will align with one content item and one science practice. Science practices are the skills needed for scientific reasoning in textual and quantitative areas.

How to Use This Book

GED® Test Science Flash Review is designed to help you prepare for and succeed on the official exam, where a strong knowledge of science fundamentals is essential. This book contains more than 600 of the exam's most commonly covered scientific concepts, images, formulas, problems, and question types. The cards are organized by science content topic for easy access.

GED® Test Science Flash Review works well as a stand-alone study tool for the science test, but it is recommended that it be used to supplement additional preparation for the exam. The following are some suggestions for making the most of this effective resource as you structure your study plan:

- Do not try to learn or memorize the 600 science concepts covered in this book all at once. Cramming is not the most effective approach to test prep. The best approach is to build a realistic study schedule that lets you review one science topic each day (refer to the table of contents to see where each new topic begins).
- Mark the topics that you have trouble with, so that they will be easy to return to later for further study.
- Make the most of this book's portability—take it with you for studying on car trips, between classes, while commuting, or whenever you have some free time.
- Keep scratch paper on hand as you make your way through the book—you might need it to work out some of the more complex problems.
- Visit the official GED® test website for additional information to help you be prepared on test day.

Best of luck on the exam—and in achieving your goals!

GED® TEST SCIENCE

....

FLASH REVIEW

Select the best answer to fill each blank from the choices that follow.

The _____ is a solid mass of iron with a temperature of about 7,000°F. The _____ is a mass of molten iron that surrounds the solid inner core. Electrical currents generated from this area produce Earth's magnetic field. The _____ is composed of silicon, oxygen, magnesium, iron, aluminum, and calcium and is about 1,750 miles thick. When parts of this layer become hot enough, they turn to slow-moving molten rock or magma. The _____ is a layer from 4 to 25 miles thick, consisting of sand and rock.
- outer core
- crust
- inner core
- rocky mantle

•••

Select the best answer to fill each blank from the choices that follow.

Sunlight _____ water from the oceans, rivers, and lakes. Living beings need water for both the outside and the inside of their cells. In fact, vertebrates (you included) are about 70% water. Evaporated water _____ to form clouds that produce rain or snow onto the earth's surface (_____).
- precipitation
- evaporates
- condenses

•••

The **inner core** is a solid mass of iron with a temperature of about 7,000°F. The **outer core** is a mass of molten iron that surrounds the solid inner core. Electrical currents generated from this area produce Earth's magnetic field. The **rocky mantle** is composed of silicon, oxygen, magnesium, iron, aluminum, and calcium and is about 1,750 miles thick. When parts of this layer become hot enough, they turn to slow-moving molten rock or magma. The **crust** is a layer from 4 to 25 miles thick, consisting of sand and rock.

. . . .

Sunlight **evaporates** water from the oceans, rivers, and lakes. Living beings need water for both the outside and the inside of their cells. In fact, vertebrates (you included) are about 70% water. Evaporated water **condenses** to form clouds that produce rain or snow onto the earth's surface (**precipitation**).

. . . .

Describe two ways that trees and other organisms contribute to the carbon cycle.

· ·

What results when tectonic plates converge?
A. mountains
B. oceans
C. trenches
D. El Niño

· ·

Explain how ocean currents can affect weather globally and locally. Answer briefly.

Sample answer (this answer may not match your own exactly).

Plants remove carbon dioxide, CO_2, from the atmosphere and convert it to sugars through photosynthesis. During respiration, organisms take O_2 from the atmosphere and replace it with CO_2.

· ·

Converging plates result in the creation of choice **A, mountains**. For example, the Andes mountain chain was formed by the Nazca Plate being pushed against the South American Plate. Tectonic plates can slide past each other, separate from each other (diverge), or come together (converge).

Oceans, such as the Atlantic, are formed by the separation of plates over millions of years. Trenches are deep channels in the ocean. El Niño is not caused by tectonic plates' movement.

· ·

Your answer will vary. Here is an example.

The Gulf Stream is an ocean current that runs from the tip of Florida and flows along the eastern United States to Newfoundland before crossing the Atlantic Ocean. Because it carries warm water, it makes Northern Europe warmer than it would be otherwise.

The oceans can affect global weather. For example, El Niño is a band of very warm ocean water that develops off the western coast of South America and can cause climatic changes. Because El Niño's warm waters feed thunderstorms, it creates increased rainfall across the eastern Pacific Ocean. Along the west coast of South America, El Niño reduces the upwelling of cold, nutrient-rich water that sustains large fish populations. The reduction in upwelling has led to fish kills off the shore of Peru. The impact of El Niño can be felt across the globe.

El Niño is
A. a current that flows from the tip of Florida along the eastern coastline of the United States.
B. the phenomenon of the sun's rays bouncing off the Earth's surface and being trapped in the atmosphere by greenhouse gases.
C. very large destructive water waves caused by earthquakes, volcanic eruptions, or landslides (not wind).
D. a band of warm ocean temperatures that develops off the west coast of South America.

· ·

What is the role of the ocean in the carbon cycle?
A. The ocean absorbs carbon from the atmosphere.
B. The ocean produces carbon dioxide.
C. Ocean currents transfer heat.
D. Water evaporates from the ocean surface.

· ·

Earthquakes are caused by
A. tsunamis.
B. global warming.
C. plate tectonics.
D. ocean currents.

The correct answer is choice **D**. El Niño develops in some years off the west coast of South America as a warm band of ocean water. The other choices describe the Gulf Stream, the greenhouse effect, and tsunamis.

. . . .

The ocean absorbs carbon from the atmosphere, choice **A**. The ocean does not produce carbon dioxide. The transfer of heat and water evaporating from the ocean surface are not related to the carbon cycle.

. . . .

Earthquakes are caused by the shifting of choice **C**, tectonic plates. Tsunamis (tidal waves) can result from earthquakes, but do not cause them. Global warming causes other natural disasters, but not earthquakes. Ocean currents do not cause earthquakes.

Compared to Earth's crust, the inner core is
A. hotter and contains more molten iron.
B. hotter and contains more solid iron.
C. hotter and contains most of Earth's mass.
D. hotter and contains mostly sand and rock.

. . . .

Solar power refers to the conversion of solar energy to another, more useful form. Sunlight can be harnessed and collected in special greenhouses. Photovoltaic cells can produce electricity when sunlight hits them. The amount of energy from the sun that reaches Earth is about 8,000 times the energy humans use. Many scientists are convinced that this form of energy will one day replace ordinary fossil fuels. In 2012, about 0.14% of all electricity generation was from solar power. This may seem like a small percentage of overall energy production, but it represents a 58% increase over 2011.

Why don't we see more of our energy coming from solar power?
A. Sunlight is always available.
B. Fossil fuels are still cheaper.
C. Fossil fuels will never run out.
D. We do not know how to produce solar power.

. . . .

Choice **B** is correct. Earth's inner core is a solid mass of iron with a temperature of about 7,000°F.

· ·

Choice **B** is correct—fossil fuels are still cheaper. All the other answers are not accurate.

· ·

Match each of the following natural resources with its correct label: renewable or nonrenewable.

Renewable Resource	Nonrenewable Resource

- coal
- gas
- oil
- plants

- sun
- water
- wind
- wood

. . . .

The greenhouse effect occurs when the sun's rays
A. **bounce off Earth's surface and are trapped in the atmosphere by greenhouse gases.**
B. **pass through the atmosphere and warm Earth's surface.**
C. **bounce off clouds and get absorbed by greenhouse gases.**
D. **move through the atmosphere and are absorbed by oceans.**

. . . .

Renewable Resource	Nonrenewable Resource
plants	oil
wind	coal
sun	gas
water	
wood	

· ·

The greenhouse effect occurs when the sun's rays bounce off Earth's surface and are trapped in the atmosphere by greenhouse gases, choice **A**. Greenhouse gases trap the sun's rays in the atmosphere, causing a temperature rise similar to how a greenhouse works.

· ·

A _____ is a system of stars, stellar dust, and dark matter bound together by gravity. The _____ comprises the sun and all planets and other objects that orbit it (including Earth).

. . . .

Explain why the northern hemisphere experiences warming in the summer. Answer briefly.

. . . .

The length of an Earth day is determined by the time it takes for one
A. Earth rotation.
B. Earth revolution.
C. sun rotation.
D. sun revolution.

A **galaxy** is a system of stars, stellar dust, and dark matter bound together by gravity, with a black hole at the center (sometimes). The **solar system** comprises the sun and all planets and other objects that orbit it (including Earth).

. . . .

Answers will vary. Here is an example.

The tilt of Earth causes the sun to hit the earth differently at different points in its revolution.

Because of the tilt of Earth's axis, we experience spring, summer, fall, and winter. We experience summer in the northern hemisphere when Earth is on the part of its orbit where the northern hemisphere is oriented toward the sun and therefore the sun rises higher in the sky and is above the horizon longer, and its rays strike the ground more directly.

Conversely, in winter in the northern hemisphere, the hemisphere is tilted away from the sun, the sun rises low in the sky and is above the horizon for a shorter period, and its rays strike the ground more obliquely.

. . . .

The correct answer is choice **A**, **Earth rotation**. Earth spins (rotates) on its axis once every 23 hours and 56 minutes. This causes day and night, and makes most extraterrestrial objects seem to move around the sky in about one day.

GED® TEST SCIENCE FLASH REVIEW

The length of an Earth year is determined by the time it takes for one
A. Earth rotation.
B. Earth revolution.
C. sun rotation.
D. sun revolution.

. . . .

What happens when the moon moves between Earth and the sun?
A. solar eclipse
B. lunar eclipse
C. night
D. solar flares

. . . .

What happens when Earth moves between the moon and sun?
A. solar eclipse
B. lunar eclipse
C. night
D. solar flares

The correct answer is choice **B, Earth revolution**. Earth revolves around the sun, in an elliptical (but nearly circular) orbit, once a year. Earth moves about 67,000 miles per hour (107,000 km/hr) in its orbit. Earth moves around the center of the Earth-moon system once a month. Earth's revolution around the sun takes much longer than its rotation on its axis. One complete revolution takes 365.24 days, or one year. The movement of the sun does not determine the length of an Earth year.

· ·

The correct answer is choice **A, solar eclipse**. The moon eclipses the sun when it is between Earth and the sun.

· ·

The correct answer is choice **B, lunar eclipse**. A lunar eclipse occurs when Earth moves between the sun and moon.

What happens to the surface of the earth when Earth rotates?
A. solar eclipse
B. lunar eclipse
C. night
D. solar flares

. . . .

What happens when the sun gives off large energy emissions?
A. solar eclipse
B. lunar eclipse
C. night
D. solar flares

. . . .

The correct answer is choice **C, night**. Night occurs due to Earth's rotation.

· ·

The correct answer is choice **D, solar flares**. Solar flares are large emissions of energy from the sun.

· ·

GED® TEST SCIENCE FLASH REVIEW

Where on the graphic would the moon need to be located in order to create a solar eclipse?

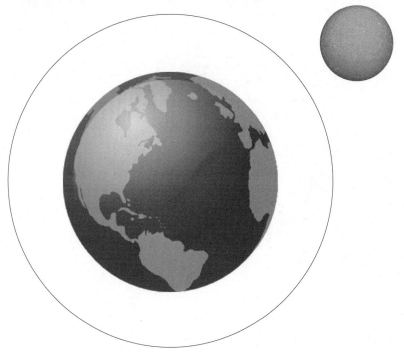

. . . .

Which of the following most accurately explains why the northern hemisphere experiences warming in summer?
A. The northern hemisphere is closer to the sun in summer than in winter.
B. The northern hemisphere experiences longer days in summer.
C. The northern hemisphere is tilted away from the sun in summer.
D. Earth's tilt on its axis causes the sun's rays to hit the northern hemisphere more directly in summer than in winter.

. . . .

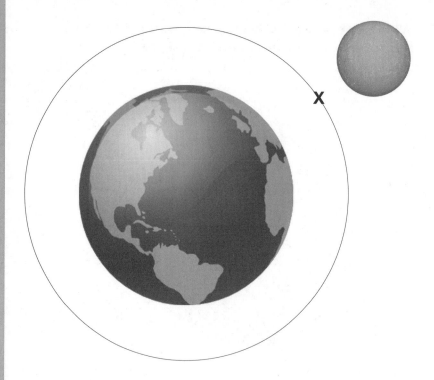

A solar eclipse occurs when the moon eclipses the sun and is directly between Earth and the sun.

· ·

Earth's tilt on its axis causes the sun's rays to hit the northern hemisphere more directly in summer than in winter, choice **D**.

· ·

Pluto is no longer considered a planet because it
A. does not orbit the sun.
B. is too small.
C. is part of an asteroid belt.
D. does not have a moon.

· ·

Pluto is part of an asteroid belt, choice **C**. It does orbit the sun as part of the Kuiper asteroid belt along with other large asteroids. Size is unrelated to designation as a planet, and Pluto has five known moons.

Kenya is a country located on the eastern edge of the African continent.

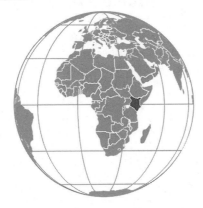

The graph shows the number of hours during which the sun is visible in Kenya for each month.

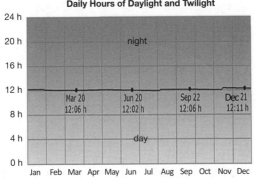

Which statement correctly explains the lack of variation in daylight hours over the course of the year?

A. The length of the day is not dependent on daylight saving time.

B. Kenya receives direct sun all year long because it is on the equator.

C. Countries in the northern and southern hemispheres have opposite seasons.

D. Earth's rotation places Kenya an equal distance from the sun during spring and fall.

Kenya receives direct sun all year long because it is on the equator, choice **B**. The tilt of Earth's axis does not substantially change the length of daily exposure of equatorial countries to the sun. Thus, the length of the day does not vary substantially over the course of the year.

Daylight saving time is the practice of advancing clocks during the lighter months so that evenings have more daylight and mornings have less. In equatorial countries, such as Kenya, there is little variation between daylight and morning hours, and there is no observation of daylight saving time.

The difference of seasons in opposing hemispheres is due to the tilt of Earth's axis and the proximity of the hemisphere to the sun. In winter, the northern hemisphere is tilted away from the sun. During winter months, the hemispheres will also experience shorter daylight hours. Kenya, an equatorial country, experiences little variance in daylight hours.

It is true that equatorial countries such as Kenya will not change position with relation to the sun in fall and spring as Earth rotates. However, this does not correctly explain the lack of variation in daylight hours over the course of an entire year.

Which of the following is considered a renewable natural resource?
A. coal
B. natural gas
C. wind
D. oil

. . . .

Earth rotates on its _____ once every _____ and makes one complete revolution around the sun once every _____.

. . . .

Ocean currents can impact weather globally. Evidence of the effect of ocean currents on global weather can be seen in
A. earthquakes.
B. volcanoes.
C. tornados.
D. El Niño.

The correct answer is choice **C, wind**. A renewable natural resource, such as wind, is one that cannot be depleted. Oil is considered a nonrenewable natural resource as our planet has only a finite amount of it. The other choices are also examples of nonrenewable natural resources because they can be depleted.

· ·

Earth rotates on its **axis** once every **day** and makes one complete revolution around the sun once every **year**.

· ·

The correct answer is choice **D, El Niño**. El Niño is a band of very warm ocean water that develops off the western coast of South America and can cause climatic changes across the planet. Because El Niño's warm waters feed thunderstorms, it creates increased rainfall across the eastern Pacific Ocean, higher temperatures in western Canada and the upper plains of the United States, and colder temperatures in the southern United States. In contrast to the flooding rains experienced in South America, the eastern coast of Africa can experience severe drought during an El Niño event. Earthquakes, volcanoes, and tornados are not related to ocean currents and do not have a global impact on weather.

Select the best answer to fill each blank from the choices (that follow).

Converging tectonic plates create _____ or island systems. When tectonic plates diverge, _____ are created.

- mountains
- cliffs
- oceans
- faults

· ·

The sun's rays bounce off the earth's surface and are trapped in the atmosphere. This is referred to as the _____ effect.

· ·

Tsunamis can be caused by
A. earthquakes.
B. wind.
C. global warming.
D. ocean currents.

Converging tectonic plates create **mountains** or island systems. When tectonic plates diverge, **oceans** are created.

. . . .

The sun's rays bounce off the earth's surface and are trapped in the atmosphere. This is referred to as the **greenhouse** effect.

. . . .

The correct answer is choice **A**, **earthquakes**. Tsunamis are very large, destructive water waves that are caused by earthquakes, volcanic eruptions, or landslides. Tsunamis used to be called "tidal waves" because they resembled a rising tide, but they have nothing to do with tides or ocean currents.

The high heat at Earth's core is a combination of three factors. Select the correct three factors from the following choices.

- residual heat from Earth's formation
- heat from the sun's formation
- frictional heating, caused by denser parts of the core moving toward the center
- heat from the friction of the tectonic plates grinding together
- residual heat from the impact with another planet in the formation of the moon
- nuclear fission occurring within the inner core
- decay of radioactive elements, such as uranium, in the core

. . . .

Is this image correctly labeled?

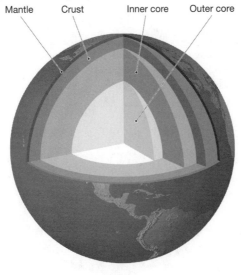

- residual heat from Earth's formation
- frictional heating, caused by denser parts of the core moving toward the center
- decay of radioactive elements, such as uranium, in the core.

· ·

No. The inner core is the center of the earth and is surrounded by the outer core. The mantle is underneath the crust, which is the outermost layer of Earth.

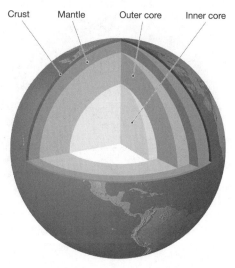

Crust   Mantle   Outer core   Inner core

· ·

Place the following gases that exist in Earth's atmosphere in order of greatest to least amounts:
- oxygen
- nitrogen
- water vapor
- small amount of other gases

. . . .

Place the following layers of the atmosphere in order from farthest to closest to the planet's surface:
- troposphere
- mesosphere
- thermosphere
- stratosphere

. . . .

What is the general order in which the following processes occur?
- evaporation of water
- precipitation
- condensation into clouds

GED® TEST SCIENCE FLASH REVIEW

The correct order is:

- nitrogen
- oxygen
- water vapor
- small amount of other gases

· ·

The correct order is:

- thermosphere
- mesosphere
- stratosphere
- troposphere

· ·

1. Evaporation of water leads to
2. condensation into clouds, which leads to
3. precipitation, which will lead back to evaporation of water.

What is the correct order of the following steps in the carbon cycle?
- These organisms release carbon dioxide back into the atmosphere when they breathe.
- Plants convert carbon dioxide to sugars through photosynthesis.
- Plants remove carbon dioxide from the atmosphere.
- Bicarbonate ions (HCO_3^-) settle on the ocean floor and form sedimentary rock.
- The sugar in plants enters the food chain, first reaching herbivores, then carnivores, and finally scavengers and decomposers.

. . . .

Which of the following statements is NOT true about fossil fuels?
A. Fossil fuels come from the carbon of organisms that lived millions of years ago.
B. Burning fossil fuel releases energy, which is why these fuels are used to power machines.
C. When fossil fuels burn, carbon dioxide is released into the atmosphere and causes global warming.
D. Fossil fuels are one of the main renewable resources in our environment.

. . . .

Select the best answer to fill the blank from the choices that follow.

Since the Industrial Revolution, when the consumption of energy to power machinery began to substantially expand, people have increased the concentration of carbon dioxide in the atmosphere by _____ by burning fossil fuels and cutting down forests that absorb carbon dioxide.
- 10%
- 30%
- 50%
- 70%

- Plants remove carbon dioxide from the atmosphere.

- Plants convert carbon dioxide to sugars through photosynthesis.

- The sugar in plants enters the food chain, first reaching herbivores, then carnivores, and finally scavengers and decomposers.

- All these organisms release carbon dioxide back into the atmosphere when they breathe.

- Bicarbonate ions (HCO_3^-) settle on the ocean floor and form sedimentary rock.

• •

Choice **D** is NOT true. Fossil fuels are not a renewable resource, as they are the carbon of organisms that lived millions of years ago.

• •

Since the Industrial Revolution, when the consumption of energy to power machinery began to substantially expand, people have increased the concentration of carbon dioxide in the atmosphere by **30%** by burning fossil fuels and cutting down forests that absorb carbon dioxide.

Which of the following gases is released by burning fossil fuels and forests and is a major component of acid rain?
A. nitric oxide
B. calcium oxide
C. manganese
D. hydrogen peroxide

· ·

Earth's upper mantle and crust are part of the
_____.

· ·

What causes the motion of the plates of Earth's crust? What is the name of this process?

GED® TEST SCIENCE FLASH REVIEW

The correct answer is choice **A, nitric oxide,** which is released and becomes nitric acid within acid rain.

· ·

Earth's upper mantle and crust are part of the **lithosphere**.

· ·

The motion of the plates of Earth's crust is caused by **convection (heat)**. This process is called **plate tectonics**.

When the plates move, they cause several familiar geological events to occur. Name one of these events.

. . . .

When one plate slides under another when the two plates meet, what is it called?
A. conduction
B. subverted
C. convection
D. subduction

. . . .

_____ is created when a plate is pushed toward the planet's core.

Volcanoes and **earthquakes** are caused when tectonic plates move.

• •

The correct answer is choice **D**, **subduction**.

• •

Magma is created when a plate is pushed toward the planet's core.

What familiar part of the planet is created by two plates coming together?

. . . .

What familiar part of the planet is created by two plates moving away from each other?

. . . .

Ocean currents are caused by several factors. Which of the following options is NOT a cause of ocean currents?
A. the rise and fall of tides
B. precipitation
C. wind currents
D. density differences in water due to temperature and salinity in different parts of the ocean

mountains

· ·

oceans

· ·

The correct answer is choice **B**. Precipitation does not cause ocean currents, but the other three factors do cause them.

What is El Niño?
A. a tsunami
B. a fault line
C. an ocean current
D. a thunderstorm

. . . .

What is the name of the process that moves water directly from bodies of water into the atmosphere?
A. infiltration
B. evaporation
C. desublimation
D. condensation

. . . .

Which way does water move during infiltration?
A. from the air into the ground
B. from the ground up to the surface
C. from the surface down into the ground
D. from the surface into the air

El Niño is choice **C, an ocean current**.

. . . .

The correct answer is choice **B, evaporation**.

. . . .

The correct answer is choice **C**, from the surface down into the ground. Melting ice and snow on the earth's surface penetrate or infiltrate into the ground.

Which of the choices matches the following description?

They can erode topsoil, destroy trees, grass, and crops, and even wash away homes. They can also contribute to the spread of disease by overflowing sewage and waste disposal infrastructure. The results of this natural hazard can take years to repair.

A. floods
B. hurricanes
C. tsunamis
D. droughts

· ·

Which of the choices matches the following description?

They can tear up the land, produce rockslides, and cause flooding if a river is redirected. The effects of this natural hazard in a big city can be devastating.

A. hurricanes
B. tsunamis
C. earthquakes
D. droughts

· ·

Which of the choices matches the following description?

They are also known as tropical cyclones—a rapidly rotating storm system with a low-pressure center, strong winds, and a spiral arrangement of thunderstorms that produce heavy rain. They form over large bodies of relatively warm water. This natural hazard can wreak havoc along coasts, destroying plants, trees, and highways.

A. floods
B. hurricanes
C. tsunamis
D. droughts

Choice **A**, **floods**, can erode topsoil, destroy trees, grass, and crops, and even tear down homes. Floods can also contribute to the spread of disease by damaging sewage and waste disposal infrastructure. The results of a flood can take years to repair.

. . . .

Choice **C**, **earthquakes**, can tear up the land, produce rockslides, and cause flooding if a river is redirected. The effects of an earthquake in a big city can be devastating.

. . . .

Choice **B**, **hurricanes**, are also known as tropical cyclones. A tropical cyclone is a rapidly rotating storm system with a low-pressure center, strong winds, and a spiral arrangement of thunderstorms that produce heavy rain. They form over large bodies of relatively warm water. Hurricanes can wreak havoc along coasts, destroying plants, trees, and highways.

Which of the choices matches the following description?

They are very large, destructive water waves caused by earthquakes, volcanic eruptions, or landslides (not wind). This natural hazard used to be called tidal waves because they resembled a rising tide, but they have nothing to do with tides.

A. floods
B. hurricanes
C. tsunamis
D. droughts

. . . .

Which of the choices matches the following description?

It occurs when an area receives substantially less precipitation than normal. This natural hazard can be designated after 15 days of reduced rainfall. Significant and sustained instances can impact crops and livestock and result in widespread food shortage, malnutrition, and famine.

A. flood
B. hurricane
C. tsunami
D. drought

. . . .

Describe what a *natural resource* is in your own words.

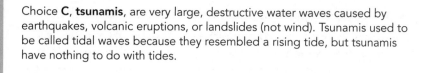

Choice **C**, **tsunamis**, are very large, destructive water waves caused by earthquakes, volcanic eruptions, or landslides (not wind). Tsunamis used to be called tidal waves because they resembled a rising tide, but tsunamis have nothing to do with tides.

. . . .

Choice **D**, **drought**, occurs when an area receives substantially less precipitation than normal. Droughts can be designated after 15 days with reduced rainfall. Significant and sustained droughts can impact crops and livestock and result in widespread food shortage, malnutrition, and famine.

. . . .

Sample answer (this answer may not match your own exactly).

Air, water, sunlight, topsoil, and plant and animal life are examples of Earth's natural resources. Natural resources occur and exist in nature and are used by humans for every aspect of survival.

The passing of one object in space through the shadow of another object is called an eclipse. The orbits of the moon and Earth in relation to the sun cause both solar and lunar eclipses to occur. During a solar eclipse, the specific alignment of these three objects causes the moon to cast a shadow on Earth. During a lunar eclipse, the alignment causes Earth to cast a shadow on the moon.

The following diagram shows the sun, Earth, and moon during a lunar eclipse. Where on the image would the moon need to be for a solar eclipse?

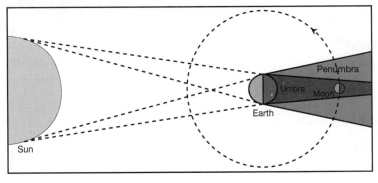

In order for an eclipse to occur, the sun, Earth, and moon must be aligned in a particular way. When Earth is positioned between the sun and the moon, Earth will prevent sunlight from reaching the moon. This is a lunar eclipse. When the moon is positioned between the sun and Earth, the moon will prevent sunlight from reaching a portion of Earth. This is a solar eclipse.

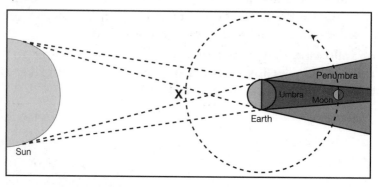

On the diagram, the moon has reached the position in its orbit that is in Earth's shadow, resulting in a lunar eclipse. From its current position on the diagram, the moon would need to travel 180° (or halfway) around its orbit to produce a solar eclipse. In this new position, the moon would cast a shadow on Earth.

This chart illustrates how the color of the light emitted by a star is dependent on the star's temperature.

Class	Color	Surface Temp. (K)
O	Blue	> 25,000 K
B	Blue-white	11,000–25,000 K
A	White	7,500–11,000 K
F	White	6,000–7,500 K
G	Yellow	5,000–6,000 K
K	Orange	3,500–5,000 K
M	Red	< 3,500 K

Which of the following statements is supported by the data in the table?
A. In general, white stars are hotter than blue-white stars.
B. A star with a surface temperature of 3,700 K produces red light.
C. Yellow light is produced by stars within the narrowest temperature range.
D. The highest known surface temperature of a star is 25,000 K.

GED® TEST SCIENCE FLASH REVIEW

The correct answer is choice **C**. Range can be determined by calculating the difference between the lowest and highest values in a data set. The table shows that the temperature of a yellow star is between 5,000 K and 6,000 K. This is a range of 1,000 K, which is the smallest (or narrowest) range listed in the table.

White stars have a maximum temperature of 11,000 K, which is the minimum temperature of blue-white stars.

Red stars have a maximum temperature of 3,500 K; a star with a temperature of 3,700 K would be within the range of an orange star.

The table does not provide information about the highest surface temperature recorded for a star, but indicates that blue stars have temperatures higher than 25,000 K.

This diagram illustrates the structure of an ocean wave.

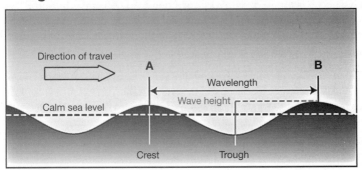

The period of a wave is the time required for the wave crest at point A to reach point B. The wave period can also be described as the amount of time required for a wave to do which of the following?

A. reach the shoreline

B. travel one wavelength

C. return to calm sea level

D. travel from crest to trough

The correct answer is choice **B**. In the context of this ocean wave diagram, a wavelength is the horizontal distance between two crests (A and B). Using the given definition of wave period, it can be determined that the wave period is the amount of time required to travel one wavelength.

A shoreline is not shown or mentioned in the diagram.

Wave period relates to the horizontal movement of a wave, while calm sea level is a reference point used to measure the vertical movement of a wave. Also, in the diagram, points A and B used to measure wave period are both crests.

The time required to travel from crest to trough would be half of a wave period.

The U.S. Geological Survey (USGS) tracks the annual occurrence and effects of natural hazards in the United States. Based on its data, the USGS has calculated the probability of a natural hazard occurring in any given year that would cause 10 or more fatalities. The following table lists the probabilities for the four most commonly occurring natural hazards.

Event	Probability of an annual event with ≥10 fatalities in the United States
Earthquake	0.11
Hurricane	0.39
Flood	0.86
Tornado	0.96

0 = no chance of occurring / 1 = 100% chance of occurring

What is the probability of a hurricane and a tornado, each causing 10 or more fatalities, both occurring in the same year?

A. 0
B. 0.37
C. 0.96
D. 1.35

. . . .

The correct answer is choice **B**. A hurricane and tornado with ≥10 fatalities each occurring in the same year would be considered a compound event, because two events are occurring together. The probability of a compound event can be determined by multiplying the probabilities of each event occurring individually. The probability of a hurricane (0.39) multiplied by the probability of a tornado (0.96) provides a compound probability of 0.3744.

A probability of 0 indicates that there is no chance of an event occurring. Since there is a possibility of a hurricane and a possibility of a tornado occurring individually, there is also a possibility for both events occurring in the same year.

A probability of 0.96 is the probability of a tornado alone occurring during any given year. The probability of both a tornado and a hurricane occurring in the same year would be much lower because the probability of a hurricane is much lower (0.39) than the probability of a tornado (0.96).

A probability greater than 1 indicates that an event is guaranteed to occur. Since the individual probabilities of a hurricane or tornado occurring are both less than 1, the probability of both events occurring in the same year would also be less than 1.

The U.S. Geological Survey (USGS) tracks the annual occurrence and effects of natural hazards in the United States. Based on its data, the USGS has calculated the probability of a natural hazard occurring in any given year that would cause 10 or more fatalities. The table lists the probabilities for the four most commonly occurring natural hazards.

Event	Probability of an annual event with ≥10 fatalities in the United States
Earthquake	0.11
Hurricane	0.39
Flood	0.86
Tornado	0.96

0 = no chance of occurring / 1 = 100% chance of occurring

Write the appropriate natural hazard from the table on the line in the passage.

A boundary between the Pacific and North American tectonic plates lies along the west coast of the continental United States. The probability of a(n) _____ with 10 or more fatalities is much higher in this region than the probability for the United States as a whole.

. . . .

The natural hazard that best completes this statement is **earthquake**. Earth's crust is made up of tectonic plates. The location where two or more tectonic plates meet is called a plate boundary. When the built up pressure at a plate boundary becomes too great, energy is released in the form of an earthquake.

Earthquakes can be expected to occur most frequently along plate boundaries. Since the west coast of the continental United States lies on a plate boundary, the probability of an earthquake occurring in this region can be predicted to be much higher than the probability for the United States as a whole, most of which does not lie on plate boundaries.

The occurrence of hurricanes, floods, and tornadoes is not specifically tied to the activity of tectonic plates. An increase in the probability of any of these natural hazards along a plate boundary as compared to the United States as a whole is not a reasonable prediction.

Information about five different fuel sources is listed in the following table.

	Energy Content (kJ/g)	CO_2 Released (mol/10^3kJ)
Hydrogen	120	0
Natural gas	51.6	1.2
Petroleum	43.6	1.6
Coal	39.3	2.0
Ethanol	27.3	1.6

Which factual statement is supported by the data in the table?

A. All cars will be fueled by hydrogen cells in the future.
B. Petroleum is a better fuel source for cars than ethanol.
C. Natural gas is too expensive to use as a fuel source for cars.
D. Ethanol fuel provides a car with less energy per gram than petroleum.

. . . .

The correct answer is choice **D**. This statement is supported by the data in the table. The energy content of ethanol is 27.3 kJ/g, about 16 kJ/g less than the energy content of petroleum (43.6 kJ/g).

The first statement is speculation based on data from the table. According to the table, hydrogen has the greatest energy content and releases no carbon dioxide. Although this data supports the speculation that cars may be fueled by hydrogen cells in the future, this statement is no guarantee. Also, although this data can be used to support the judgment that petroleum is a better fuel source than ethanol, that statement is an opinion rather than a fact. As well, while the data in the table suggests that natural gas is a relatively efficient and clean fuel source, the statement is speculation because no information is provided about the cost of natural gas.

Natural gas, petroleum, and coal are fossil fuels. Ethanol is derived from biomass.

Information about five different fuel sources is listed in the following table.

	Energy Content (kJ/g)	CO_2 Released (mol/10^3kJ)
Hydrogen	120	0
Natural gas	51.6	1.2
Petroleum	43.6	1.6
Coal	39.3	2.0
Ethanol	27.3	1.6

Based on the data in the table, what is the best estimate of the energy content of fossil fuels?
A. 40 kJ/g
B. 42 kJ/g
C. 45 kJ/g
D. 50 kJ/g

. . . .

The correct answer is choice **C**. The passage identifies natural gas, petroleum, and coal as fossil fuels, because each is derived from the fossil remains of organisms. The energy content of each fossil fuel can be approximated to 50 kJ/g, 45 kJ/g, and 40 kJ/g, respectively. This provides an estimated average energy content of 45 kJ/g.

Choice **A**, 40 kJ/g, would be an appropriate estimate for the energy content of coal, not for the energy content of all three fossil fuels. Choice **B**, 42 kJ/g, would be an appropriate estimate for the energy content of petroleum and coal without including natural gas, which is also a fossil fuel. Choice **C**, 50 kJ/g, would be an appropriate estimate for the energy content of natural gas, not for the energy content of all three fossil fuels.

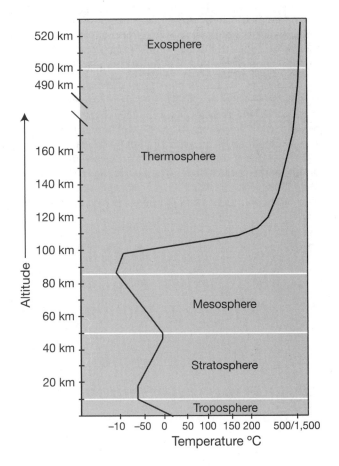

According to the graph, in which atmospheric layers does temperature decrease as altitude increases?
A. mesosphere and exosphere
B. troposphere and thermosphere
C. stratosphere and thermosphere
D. troposphere and mesosphere

GED® TEST SCIENCE FLASH REVIEW

The correct answer is choice **D**. In the graph, temperature increases to the right and altitude increases upward. Any portion of the graph that has a negative slope, or slopes to the left, indicates a decrease in temperature. The graph has a negative slope in the troposphere and mesosphere layers.

The graph has a negative slope within the mesosphere, but a slight positive slope in the exosphere. This means that temperature decreases as altitude increases in the mesosphere, but increases with altitude in the exosphere. The graph has a negative slope within the troposphere, but a positive slope in the thermosphere. Even though the slope is not constant within the thermosphere, the slope remains positive within this layer. This means that temperature decreases in the troposphere, but increases in the thermosphere. The graph has a positive slope within both the stratosphere and thermosphere. This means that temperature increases with altitude in both layers.

Surface currents in the ocean are classified as warm or cold currents. In general, warm currents tend to travel from the equator toward the poles along the eastern coast of continents. Cold currents tend to travel from the poles toward the equator along the western coast of continents. The map shows the major surface ocean currents of the world.

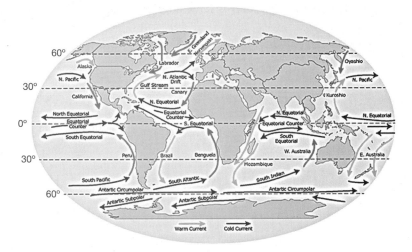

Based on the statement and the map, which of the following statements about the Alaska current is true?

A. The Alaska current is a typical cold current because it travels along the western coast of the continent.

B. The Alaska current is not a true surface current because it does not follow the general pattern of surface currents.

C. The Alaska current is an exception to the general pattern because warm currents typically travel along the eastern coast of continents.

D. The Alaska current transports water from the North Pole toward the equator because it travels along the western coast of the continent.

The correct answer is choice **C**. The Alaska current is a warm current. The passage states that warm currents typically travel along the eastern coast of continents, but the Alaska current travels along the western coast of North America.

Although the Alaska current does travel along the western coast of the continent, the map key indicates that it is a warm current. The Alaska current does not follow the typical pattern for a warm current, but is identified as a surface current on the map. Warm currents typically transport warm water originating near the equator toward the poles.

There are two kinds of natural resources: renewable and nonrenewable resources. Which kind is crude oil?

. . . .

There are two kinds of natural resources: renewable and nonrenewable resources. Which kind is uranium?

. . . .

There are two kinds of natural resources: renewable and nonrenewable resources. Which kind is coal?

Crude oil is a fossil fuel and so is a **nonrenewable resource**.

. . . .

Uranium is a nuclear fuel and so is a **nonrenewable resource**.

. . . .

Coal is a fossil fuel and so is a **nonrenewable resource**.

There are two kinds of natural resources: renewable and nonrenewable resources. Which kind is wind power?

. . . .

There are two kinds of natural resources: renewable and nonrenewable resources. Which kind is pea starch?

. . . .

There are two kinds of natural resources: renewable and nonrenewable resources. Which kind is sugarcane?

Wind power is a constant and therefore is a **renewable resource**.

· ·

Pea starch is created from a growing plant and can be used to make bioplastics, so it is a **renewable resource**.

· ·

Sugarcane is a growing plant and can be used in making ethanol as fuel, so it is a **renewable resource**.

There are two kinds of natural resources: renewable and nonrenewable resources. Which kind is jatropha?

· ·

What is the term for the planet's huge variety of plants and animals?

· ·

Oceans cover what percentage of Earth's surface?
A. 50%
B. 32%
C. 70%
D. 94%

Jatropha is a weed that can be made into biodiesel fuel, so it is a **renewable resource**.

· ·

biodiversity

· ·

Oceans cover choice **C**, **70%** of Earth's surface.

Approximately what percentage of the total water on Earth is in the oceans?

A. 43%

B. 97%

C. 73%

D. 58%

. . . .

Global climate change is having significant negative effects on oceans, which absorb about one-fourth of the carbon dioxide (CO_2) emitted from human activities. This phenomenon is called _____.

. . . .

When CO_2 is absorbed by the ocean, it interacts with saltwater to form carbonic acid. As CO_2 levels in the atmosphere continue to increase, levels of carbonic acid in oceans also increase. This ocean acidification will harm plankton, adversely affect shellfish larvae, hinder the ability of corals to build new reefs, and cause serious food chain disruptions.

Coral reefs and estuaries (salty or brackish freshwater that runs into the ocean) sustain 75 percent of all commercial fish and shellfish during some point of their life cycles. One in six people on Earth depend on ocean fish for their primary source of protein.

How might a graph show how increasing quantities of CO_2 in the oceans affect humans?

Oceans contain more than choice **B**, **97%** of the total water on Earth.

. . . .

This phenomenon is called **carbon sink**. Oceans contain 500 times more carbon than the atmosphere.

. . . .

Answers may vary.

The graph would show increasing quantities of CO_2 over time, and also the drop in fish replenishment and drop in protein intake for many humans.

As a result of warmer global temperatures, oceans are warming worldwide, producing adverse effects. Which of the following is NOT an adverse effect of warmer oceans?

A. The ice sheets in the Arctic are growing, with negative consequences for many species of marine mammals that live there.
B. Challenges to ocean creatures include increased marine diseases, invasive species, and the death of coral reefs.
C. Larger and more frequent storms are accelerating shoreline erosion.
D. Sea-level rise causes habitat loss and risk to islands and coastal homes.

. . . .

There are three ways that energy is transferred between Earth's surface and atmosphere. What is one of those ways?

. . . .

Carbon dioxide and other gases in the atmosphere can trap solar energy in a process known as what?

The correct answer is choice **A**. The statement that the ice sheets in the Arctic are growing, with negative consequences for many species of marine mammals that live there, is not true. The ice sheets in the Arctic are actually melting, which has a negative effect on the mammals living there.

. . . .

Conduction, **convection**, and **radiation** are all ways energy is transferred.

. . . .

Carbon dioxide and other gases in the atmosphere can trap solar energy in a process known as the **greenhouse effect**.

Solar energy technology is catching up. Which of the following statements about this is NOT accurate?
A. Solar plants are now being constructed in many areas in the United States and throughout the world.
B. Solar plants are being constructed in large floating barges on the oceans.
C. In 2012, about 0.14% of all electricity generation was from solar power. This may seem like a small percentage of overall energy production, but it represents a 58% increase over 2011.
D. Many people are finding employment in the solar industry. In 2012, there were more than 119,000 solar workers in the United States, a 13.2% increase over employment totals in 2011.

. . . .

Wind power refers to the conversion of wind energy into a usable form of energy. Which of the following is NOT true?
A. Large wind farms consist of hundreds of individual wind turbines, which are connected to the electric power grid. There are wind farms on land and in oceans.
B. Some countries are far ahead of the United States in harnessing wind power for energy. Denmark generates more than a quarter of its electricity from wind.
C. Tilting a windmill has become a regular practice for wind energy conversion.
D. In 2010, wind energy production was more than 2.5% of total worldwide electricity usage. The cost per unit of energy produced is similar to the cost of new coal and natural gas installations.

. . . .

Choice **B** is not an accurate statement. The other three statements are accurate regarding solar energy technology catching up.

· ·

Choice **C** is not a true statement about wind power.

· ·

GED® TEST SCIENCE FLASH REVIEW

_____ is heat energy produced in the rock and fluids beneath Earth's crust. It can be found from shallow ground to several miles below the surface, and even farther down to the extremely hot molten rock called magma. Deep wells are drilled into underground reservoirs to tap steam and very hot water to drive turbines linked to electric generators.

. . . .

Summarize the concept of the Big Bang Theory in terms of how it relates to the structure of the universe.

. . . .

What are millions of stars bound near each other by gravity called?

Geothermal energy is heat energy produced in the rock and fluids beneath Earth's crust. It can be found from shallow ground to several miles below the surface, and even farther down to the extremely hot molten rock called magma. Deep wells are drilled into underground reservoirs to tap steam and very hot water to drive turbines linked to electric generators.

. . . .

Answers may vary.

The Big Bang Theory is the theory that the universe originally was compressed into a tiny, high-density, high-pressure point in space, and when it blew out in a bang, the universe expanded outward and has continued since.

. . . .

These groupings of stars are called **galaxies**.

What is Earth's galaxy called?

. . . .

What is the Big Dipper?

. . . .

What is one of the characteristics of a planet that makes it a planet?

The Milky Way

· ·

a constellation

· ·

A **planet** is a celestial body that has enough mass to be spherical, orbits the sun or other stars in other solar systems, and is not part of an asteroid belt.

What was one of the characteristics that caused Pluto to lose its status as one of the planets of our solar system?

. . . .

Which of the following statements about comets is **NOT** true?

A. A comet is a small, icy celestial body that, when passing close to the sun, may display a tail.

B. Comet tails are caused by solar radiation and solar wind.

C. Comets range from a few hundred meters to tens of kilometers across, and are composed of loose collections of quartz, diamond, and silicate.

D. The orbit of a comet can last a few years to several hundred years. For example, Halley's comet is visible from Earth about every 75 years. Its next appearance should be in 2061.

. . . .

What is the main difference between an asteroid and a comet?

Pluto was long considered one of nine planets in Earth's solar system, but in the 1990s, astronomers learned that Pluto was not a planet in its own orbit, but part of a belt of asteroids. Because of this, astronomers voted to change Pluto's designation to **dwarf planet** in 2006.

. . . .

Choice **C** is *not* true. While the size of a comet can range from a few hundred meters to tens of kilometers across, the composition of a comet is ice, rock, and dust.

. . . .

Asteroids are similar to comets, but differ in composition. Asteroids are made up of metals and rocky materials and have no tail because they are not composed of ice. There are also millions of asteroids, some as small as dust particles. Others are as large as half a mile in diameter.

Where does the life cycle of a star begin?

. . . .

When a star is just being born, what could it be called?
A. a white dwarf
B. a protostar
C. a red giant
D. a main sequence star

. . . .

What is the longest stage of the life span of a star?
A. a white dwarf
B. a protostar
C. a red giant
D. a main sequence star

Stars begin in a place called stellar nurseries, which are a type of nebula. A **nebula** is a cloud of dust and gas, composed of about 97% hydrogen and 3% helium. Nebulae may be giant, with 1,000 to 100,000 times the mass of the sun, or smaller, with less than a few hundred times the mass of the sun.

· ·

The correct answer is choice **B**, **a protostar**. This is before the star stabilizes and while it's still gathering mass, energy, and density from the nebula in which it formed. Once it gets hot enough that the hydrogen atoms start fusing and it gathers enough mass, it moves on to the next stage of development.

· ·

The correct answer is choice **D**. When a star becomes **a main sequence star**, it stabilizes and matures into stellar adulthood. The creation phase of a star the size of Earth's sun can take up to 50 million years, but the adulthood phase then will last another 10 billion years.

Once a star the size of Earth's sun runs out of hydrogen
and its core collapses, what is its next possible stage?
A. a white dwarf
B. a protostar
C. a red giant
D. a main sequence star

. . . .

What causes things like black holes to occur?

. . . .

What is the Arctic Zone?

GED® TEST SCIENCE FLASH REVIEW

This stage would be choice **C**, the **red giant** stage. As the core collapses, it heats up and heats the upper layers of the star. These layers expand outward and the entire star gives off a cooler and redder light, which is why it's called a red giant.

· ·

Black holes are created when a very large star reaches the end of its life span at which time the following occurs:

- After the helium is gone, the star's mass is enough to fuse carbon into heavier elements such as oxygen, neon, silicon, magnesium, sulfur, and iron.

- Once the core has turned to iron, it can no longer burn. The star collapses from its own gravity. The core becomes so tightly packed that protons and electrons merge to form neutrons.

- In less than a second, the iron core, which is about the size of Earth, shrinks to a neutron core with a radius of about 6 miles (10 kilometers).

- The core heats to billions of degrees and explodes in a **supernova**, releasing large amounts of energy and material into space. The remains of the core can form a **neutron star** or a **black hole** depending on the original star's mass.

· ·

The Arctic Zone is the climatic zone near the North or South Pole characterized by long, cold winters and short, cool summers.

Refer to the following passage to answer the next five questions.

Gas exchange between the air and oceans is primarily controlled by the air-sea difference in gas concentrations. It is not unusual for there to be differences in the carbon dioxide (CO_2) levels between air and ocean because it takes about a year for surface ocean CO_2 to equilibrate with the atmospheric CO_2. Oceans hold large reservoirs of carbon that can be exchanged with the air because CO_2 reacts with water to form carbonic acid. Ocean acidification is a result of increasing atmospheric carbon dioxide levels interacting with the surface oceans. When increasing CO_2 levels change the global climate, the temperature changes impact ocean circulation; in turn, ocean circulation impacts ocean CO_2 uptake. Ocean acidification impacts marine ecosystems, which can also result in changes in the air-sea CO_2 exchange.

What is the main topic of this passage?
A. mechanisms of ocean circulation and its effects
B. ocean acidification and its consequences
C. ocean CO_2 absorption and its consequences
D. oceans and global climate change

. . . .

When carbon dioxide is absorbed by the ocean, it becomes _____.

. . . .

The correct answer is choice **C, ocean CO$_2$ absorption and its consequences**. When analyzing the subjects of each sentence, here is the breakdown:

1. Gas exchange between the air and oceans happens.

2. It is not unusual for there to be differences in carbon dioxide (CO$_2$) levels between air and ocean.

3. Oceans hold large reservoirs of carbon that can be exchanged with the air.

4. Ocean acidification is a result of increasing atmospheric carbon dioxide levels interacting with the surface oceans.

5. When increasing CO$_2$ levels change the global climate, the temperature changes impact ocean circulation.

6. Ocean acidification impacts marine ecosystems, which can also result in changes in the air-sea CO$_2$ exchange.

The majority of the subjects deal with carbon dioxide and the oceans, so the most likely main idea of this passage is ocean CO$_2$ absorption and its consequences.

· ·

When carbon dioxide is absorbed by the ocean, it becomes **carbonic acid**.

The third sentence of the passage states "CO$_2$ reacts with water to form carbonic acid."

· ·

Which choice explains how increasing atmospheric CO_2 necessarily alters atmospheric CO_2?

A. Increasing atmospheric CO_2 levels can decrease ocean acidification, which in turn puts more CO_2 into the atmosphere.

B. Increasing atmospheric CO_2 levels can decrease the ocean's reservoir of carbonic acid, thereby decreasing atmospheric CO_2.

C. Increasing atmospheric CO_2 levels can change global temperature and impact ocean circulation, which impacts ocean CO_2 uptake.

D. Increasing atmospheric CO_2 levels can directly increase ocean absorption of CO_2, thereby increasing atmospheric CO_2 levels further.

· ·

How do you find the context for the word *equilibrate* in the sentence "It is not unusual for there to be differences in the carbon dioxide (CO_2) levels between air and ocean because it takes about a year for surface ocean CO_2 to equilibrate with the atmospheric CO_2"?

· ·

How do you find the context for the phrase *ocean acidification* in the sentence "Ocean acidification is a result of increasing atmospheric carbon dioxide levels interacting with the surface oceans"?

The correct answer is choice **C**. Increasing atmospheric CO_2 levels can change global temperature and impact ocean circulation, which impacts ocean CO_2 uptake.

The next to the last sentence states, "When increasing CO_2 levels change the global climate, the temperature changes impact ocean circulation; in turn, ocean circulation impacts ocean CO_2 uptake." So, the mediator between increasing atmospheric CO_2 and its self-regulation is global temperature and oceanic circulation.

· ·

The word *differences* is the opposite and shows that *equilibrate* means to create an equal amount of CO_2 between the surface ocean and atmosphere.

· ·

The phrase *is a result of* leads to the cause of ocean acidification and relates it to carbon dioxide and the previous sentence "Oceans hold large reservoirs of carbon that can be exchanged with the air because CO_2 reacts with water to form carbonic acid."

_____

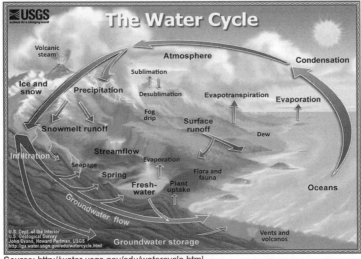

Source: http://water.usgs.gov/edu/watercycle.html

From this diagram, what would you guess that *desublimation* means?

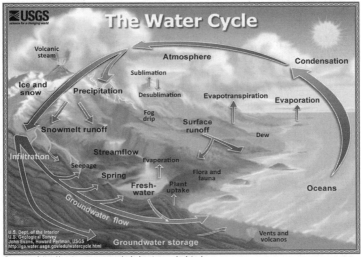

Source: http://water.usgs.gov/edu/watercycle.html

From this diagram, what would you guess that *condensation* means?

Your answer may vary.

This shows the phase change of the water vapor in the air into ice, so desublimation is the phase change of a gas into a solid.

. . . .

Your answer may vary.

This shows the change of water vapor in the air into clouds, leading to precipitation, so condensation is the phase change of a gas into a liquid.

. . . .

Which type of weather pattern would be expected with the weather front shown in the diagram?

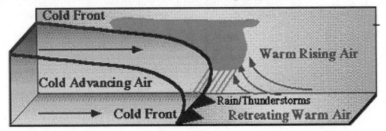

A. a long band of widespread gentle rain or snow
B. a narrow band of widespread gentle rain or snow
C. a long band of severe thunderstorms
D. a narrow band of severe thunderstorms

The correct answer is choice **D**, a narrow band of severe thunderstorms. In a cold front, the band of severe thunderstorms is narrow as the warm air rises rapidly against the steep advancing cold air mass.

· ·

The diagram shows circulation within the world's oceans. Which best describes ocean circulation patterns?

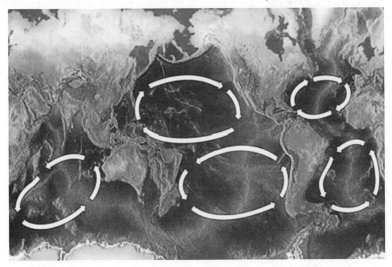

A. Currents generally move clockwise in the northern hemisphere and counterclockwise in the southern hemisphere.
B. Currents generally move clockwise in the southern hemisphere and counterclockwise in the northern hemisphere.
C. Currents generally move counterclockwise in both hemispheres.
D. Currents generally move clockwise in both hemispheres.

. . . .

The correct answer is choice **A**. Currents generally move clockwise in the northern hemisphere and counterclockwise in the southern hemisphere. The diagram shows that ocean currents do move clockwise in the northern hemisphere and counterclockwise in the southern hemisphere.

The diagram shows circulation within the world's oceans. Predict how the currents would affect the ocean and climate of the Eastern coast of North America.

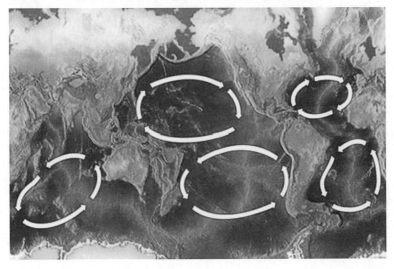

Answers may vary.

The currents would bring warmer ocean water from the equator up along the coast, directing any weather patterns of storms and hurricanes up the coast. It also makes the climate warmer than it otherwise might be if the currents were not there.

Refer to the following passage to answer the next three questions.

In 2009, the North Carolina Coastal Resources Commission (CRC) organized a science panel of expert scientists to review the published literature on sea level rise (SLR) and make projections for the state through 2100. The science panel projected that by 2100, a 0.4 m rise was certain, a 1.0 m rise was more likely, and a 1.40 m rise was possible (see graph). The panel recommended that the SLR projections be taken into consideration in future coastal planning.

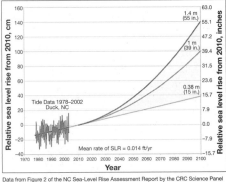

Data from Figure 2 of the NC Sea-Level Rise Assessment Report by the CRC Science Panel on Coastal Hazards, March 2010

The report's SLR projection agreed with projections from other science panels, including in Miami-Dade County (1–2 m), Rhode Island (1–1.5 m), Maine (1 m), Oregon (1.4 m), and the Puget Sound (1 m). However, it disagreed with a linear projection from historical data that SLR would be 0.2 m.

In response to the report, an advocacy group of coastal businesses and government officials from coastal counties lobbied the state legislature to consider a bill declaring that only the linear projection could be considered in any NC coastal planning. The bill was revised to ignore SLR in any coastal planning and mandated a new report from the panel, in which all data and hypotheses regarding changes in sea level (linear rise, accelerated rise, decrease, etc.) should be listed, not just those with the consensus of the scientific community; the bill was passed and signed into law in 2012.

The advocacy group cited discredited scientific studies, arguing that there was no scientific consensus on SLR, and ridiculed the science panel. The group successfully convinced the legislature and many citizens.

This passage is based on *Denying sea-level rise: How 100 centimeters divided the state of North Carolina*, by Alexander Glass and Orrin Pilkey, originally published in ©Earthmagazine.org, and *Earth Magazine*, p. 26, May 2013.

Are the claims in the article regarding sea level rise from reliable sources?

Yes. The claims were made from government science panels in North Carolina, Miami-Dade County, Rhode Island, Maine, Oregon, and the Puget Sound.

Are the sea level rise claims verified with supporting data?

. . . .

Are there a variety of sources to help establish evidence and resolve conflicting information?

. . . .

A forecast shows the chance of rain on Friday is 10%, 30%, 70%, and 50% for Miami, Los Angeles, Seattle, and Chicago, respectively. What is the probability that it will rain in all four cities on Friday?

Yes. A graph from the CRC science panel report was included.

. . . .

No. The conflicting SLR projection from historical data was mentioned, but the source was not identified. The conflict between the scientific panel's projection and the projection from historical data is a central theme of the passage.

. . . .

The correct answer is **0.0105 or 1.05%**. Here's the solution:

P(Miami) = 10% = 0.1

P(Los Angeles) = 30% = 0.3

P(Seattle) = 70% = 0.7

P(Chicago) = 50% = 0.5

P(all 4 cities) = P(Miami) $\cdot$ P(Los Angeles) $\cdot$ P(Seattle) $\cdot$ P(Chicago)

P(all 4 cities) = 0.1 $\cdot$ 0.3 $\cdot$ 0.7 $\cdot$ 0.5

P(all 4 cities) = 0.0105 = 1.05%

Carlos wants to make his home more energy efficient, and he wants an affordable and environmentally responsible solution. Carlos lives in the western United States. His house is located on a small lot in an urban neighborhood that is sparsely landscaped.

Which of these options would meet all of Carlos's needs and criteria?

A. Place solar panels on the roof.
B. Install a wind turbine in the front yard.
C. Replace an oil-fired furnace with a wood-burning stove.
D. Contact electricity companies to compare prices and negotiate rates.

. . . .

Keesha has a farm and sells her extra produce at the local farmer's market. She wants to make her business and home more energy efficient and environmentally responsible. She lives in the middle of the United States on a large plot of land in the country, with lots of flat plains around her.

Which of these options would meet all of Keesha's needs and criteria?

A. Place solar panels on the roof.
B. Install wind turbines in the fields.
C. Replace an oil-fired furnace with a wood-burning stove.
D. Contact electricity companies to compare prices and negotiate rates.

. . . .

The correct answer is choice **A**, place solar panels on the roof. Incorporating solar panels into his home would allow Carlos to use less fossil fuel energy while saving money.

· ·

The correct answer is choice **B**, install wind turbines in the fields. Installing wind turbines would allow Keesha to use less fossil fuel energy, save money, and also take advantage of the wind movement where she is located.

· ·

The chart presents information on ultraviolet radiation. It is divided into wavelength ranges identified as UVA, UVB, and UVC.

Radiation	UVA	UVB	UVC
Main human effect	Aging	Burning	
Wavelength	400 nm to 315 nm	315 nm to 280 nm	280 nm to 100 nm
% reaching Earth 12 noon	95%	5%	0%
% reaching Earth before 10 A.M. & after 2 P.M.	99%	1%	0%
% reaching Earth (average)	97%	3%	0%
NOTES		creates vitamin D	

People are most likely to be at risk of sunburn at
A. 10 A.M., because the UVA rays are the greatest.
B. 12 P.M., because more UVB rays reach the earth.
C. 2 P.M., because UVC rays are least harmful.
D. 4 P.M., because the UVA rays have less strength.

. . . .

The correct answer is choice **B**, **12:00** P.M., because more UVB rays reach the earth. UVB rays cause sunburns. The greatest percentage of UVB rays reach the earth at noon (12 P.M.), making it the most likely time of day for sunburn to happen.

The chart presents information on ultraviolet radiation. It is divided into wavelength ranges identified as UVA, UVB, and UVC.

Radiation	UVA	UVB	UVC
Main human effect	Aging	Burning	
Wavelength	400 nm to 315 nm	315 nm to 280 nm	280 nm to 100 nm
% reaching Earth 12 noon	95%	5%	0%
% reaching Earth before 10 A.M. & after 2 P.M.	99%	1%	0%
% reaching Earth (average)	97%	3%	0%
NOTES		creates vitamin D	

Based on the wavelengths noted, what can you determine about the wavelengths of UVA, UVB, and UVC?

. . . .

Answers may vary.

UVA is a longer wavelength than UVB, and UVC is the shortest of them.

Refer to the following passage to answer the next three questions.

Billions of barrels of oil are believed to be locked in soft, finely stratified sedimentary shale formations throughout the United States. Natural gas and oil companies are hard at work freeing these resources. Hydraulic fracturing, more commonly referred to as *fracking*, is a drilling process in which millions of gallons of fresh water, sand, and chemicals are injected under high pressure into a well. This cracks the existing rock and releases the natural gas and oil.

The fluids used in hydraulic fracturing, and the wastewater that comes back up the well, need to be disposed of. The safest, most cost-efficient method of disposal involves injecting the fluids into disposal wells thousands of feet underground. The wells are encased in layers of concrete and usually store the waste from several different wells. Each holds about 4.5 million gallons of chemical-laced water.

Sometimes, injections of waste into these wells cause earthquakes. These earthquakes occur as crevices, previously containing oil, are filled with water. The resulting pressure change needed to push the water underground can trigger a slip in a nearby fault line.

Based on the information in the passage, where are the natural gas deposits that are targeted by hydraulic fracturing?
A. underneath sand
B. in shale formations
C. inside concrete wells
D. below the water table

The correct answer is choice **B, in shale formations**. Soft, finely stratified sedimentary shale formations are home to billions of barrels of oil as well as natural gas.

On the map, the circles indicate locations of earthquakes caused by or related to energy technologies. The larger the circle, the larger the earthquake.

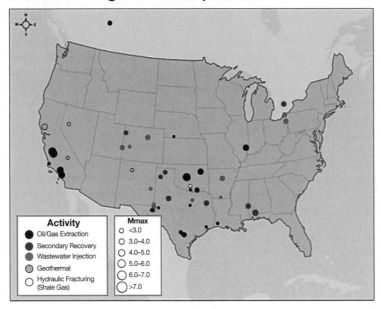

What is the activity in the key that results in earthquakes with the greatest magnitude?

. . . .

According to the information in the passage, which of the following statements best describes concerns about the possible sustainability of hydraulic fracturing?
A. Ongoing fracking could pollute the air.
B. The potential for earthquakes is increasing.
C. Fresh water supplies in shale outcroppings are scarce.
D. Gas and oil surpluses cause less reliance on wind and solar resources.

. . . .

The correct answer is **Oil/Gas Extraction**. The circles in the activity legend indicate the location of earthquakes that were "caused by or related to energy technologies. The larger the circle, the larger the earthquake." The largest circles on the map are black, which represents Oil/Gas Extraction.

· ·

The correct answer is choice **C**, fresh water supplies in shale outcroppings are scarce. Water is scarce in the regions targeted by hydraulic fracturing, and the sustainability of fresh water must be addressed. When "millions of gallons of fresh water, sand, and chemicals are injected under high pressure into a well," the reality of the vast amounts of this resource being used comes to light.

· ·

Refer to the following passage to answer the next four questions.

Ocean acidification occurs when seawater absorbs carbon dioxide from the atmosphere. This causes the water to become more acidic. Dissolved carbon dioxide increases the hydrogen ion concentration in the ocean, which decreases the ocean's pH level. Calcifying organisms such as corals, oysters, and sea urchins find it more difficult to build shells and skeletons in acidic water.

Carbon dioxide in the atmosphere comes from many sources. When humans burn oil or gas to generate power, carbon dioxide is released. Carbon dioxide is also a greenhouse gas, which means it leads to warmer temperatures on Earth's surface by trapping heat in the air.

Atmospheric CO_2 at Mauna Loa Observatory

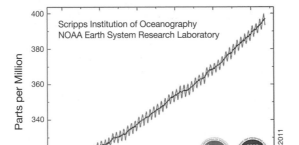

Based on the graph and the information from the passage, what year presented the lowest risk of ocean acidification?

A. 1960

B. 1970

C. 1990

D. 2010

The correct answer is choice **A, 1960**. Ocean acidification occurs when seawater absorbs carbon dioxide from the atmosphere. The point on the graph indicating the lowest concentration of atmospheric CO_2 is 1960.

Referencing the passage, which effect from carbon dioxide could have a direct negative impact on marine food webs?
A. reduced calcification of coral
B. increased air pollution from cars
C. rising sea levels from melting glaciers
D. warmer temperatures on Earth's surface

· ·

Which type of coastal erosion would be most impacted by ocean acidification?
A. abrasion
B. attrition
C. corrosion
D. hydraulic action

· ·

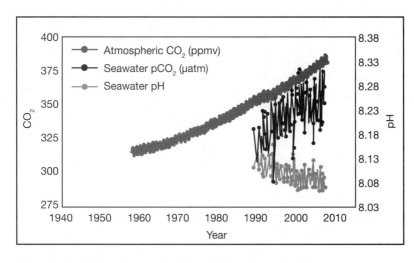

When considering both the passage and the image, overall, what statement might be inferred?
A. Ocean acidification is not a problem.
B. Before the 1990s, seawater pH did not exist.
C. Carbon dioxide comes from only one source.
D. Calcium carbonate can be dissolved by acidic water.

The correct answer is choice **A**, reduced calcification of coral. Increased acidification of ocean waters creates a poor environment for calcifying marine animals. Corals are primary consumers in marine food webs. When corals cannot properly function and they begin to die, the secondary and tertiary consumers are negatively impacted.

· ·

The correct answer is choice **C, corrosion**. The process of corrosion occurs when materials with a low pH chemically weather cliff rocks with a high pH. The increased acidity of seawater significantly contributes to the way sea cliffs break apart.

· ·

The correct answer is choice **D**. Calcium carbonate can be dissolved by acidic water. This can be determined by "Calcifying organisms such as corals, oysters, and sea urchins find it more difficult to build shells and skeletons in acidic water." Since *calcifying* has the same root as *calcium*, it seems likely that this is the true statement. The other statements are all false.

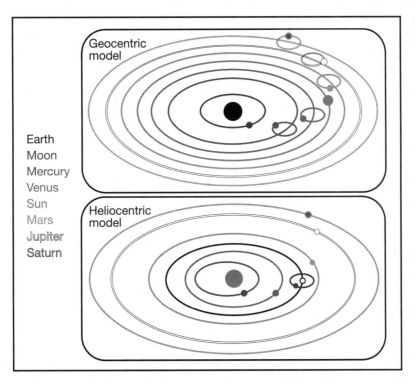

Earth
Moon
Mercury
Venus
Sun
Mars
Jupiter
Saturn

Geocentric model proposed by Ptolemy (top) and heliocentric model proposed by Copernicus (bottom)

With the two diagrams shown here, what can you determine about how Ptolemy and Copernicus saw the solar system?

. . . .

Answers may vary.

Ptolemy saw the solar system as a system with the sun and other planets orbiting Earth, while Copernicus saw the solar system as a system in which the sun was the center and Earth and other planets orbit it.

The chart presents information on ultraviolet radiation. It is divided into wavelength ranges identified as UVA, UVB, and UVC.

Radiation	UVA	UVB	UVC
Main human effect	Aging	Burning	
Wavelength	400 nm to 315 nm	315 nm to 280 nm	280 nm to 100 nm
% reaching Earth 12 noon	95%	5%	0%
% reaching Earth before 10 A.M. & after 2 P.M.	99%	1%	0%
% reaching Earth (average)	97%	3%	0%
NOTES		creates vitamin D	

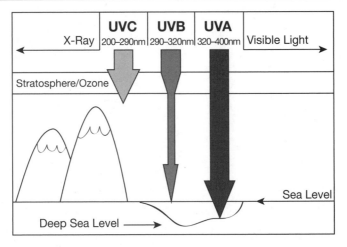

With the chart and diagram, what can you determine about UVC waves?

. . . .

Answers may vary.

UVC does not reach the surface of the earth, so does not affect humans.

Refer to the following passage to answer the next four questions.

As the world searches for alternatives to petroleum, corn-based ethanol and other biofuels derived from organic material have been considered as the perfect answer to transportation fuel problems. In fact, a U.S. government energy bill mandates that over 30 billion gallons of biofuels a year be used by the year 2020. However, separate studies released by the Nature Conservancy and Ivy League institutions reveal that ethanol may not be the best answer in the fight against global warming. They say biofuels could make things worse.

Biofuel crops, such as corn and sugarcane, remove carbon from Earth's atmosphere while they are growing. When biofuels are burned, they emit fewer greenhouse gases than fossil fuels like coal or oil. This makes biofuels almost carbon-neutral. However, studies are showing that ethanol could be even more dangerous for the environment than fossil fuels. The Ivy League study noted that clearing previously untouched land to grow biofuel crops releases long-contained carbon into the atmosphere. While planting biofuel crops in already tilled land is all right, the problem arises when farmers disturb new land to grow more sugarcane or corn. Additionally, food and feed crops are being displaced by biofuel crops. The Nature Conservancy warns that "converting rainforests, peat lands, savannas, or grasslands to produce biofuels in Brazil, Southeast Asia and the United States creates a 'biofuel carbon debt' by releasing 17 to 420 times more carbon dioxide than the fossil fuels they replace." Other negative effects include the extreme amounts of water needed for irrigation, runoffs from pesticides and fertilizers, and the natural gas used to make the fertilizers that adds to the carbon deficit.

Are the claims in the article from reliable sources?

. . . .

Are the claims in the article verified with supporting data?

. . . .

Yes. The article mentions studies released by the Nature Conservancy and Ivy League institutions. These institutions generally count as reliable and valid sources.

. . . .

This article excerpt does not include copies of the data from the studies it mentions. However, the following quote from the Nature Conservancy does provide some supporting data for the answer: "converting rainforests, peat lands, savannas, or grasslands to produce biofuels in Brazil, Southeast Asia and the United States creates a 'biofuel carbon debt' by releasing 17 to 420 times more carbon dioxide than the fossil fuels they replace."

. . . .

Are there a variety of sources to help establish evidence and resolve conflicting information?

. . . .

List at least three pieces of evidence from the passage that support the claim that ethanol is not a sustainable source of transportation fuel.

. . . .

Yes, the article cites reports from the Nature Conservancy, Ivy League institutions, and a U.S. government energy bill.

. . . .

Answers may vary.

- Clearing previously untouched land to grow biofuel crops releases long-contained carbon into the atmosphere.

- Growing biofuel crops displaces food and feed crops.

- Biofuel crops need extreme amounts of water for irrigation.

- Treating fields of biofuel crops with pesticides and fertilizers creates pollution when these chemicals run off into waterways.

- Making fertilizers for growing biofuel crops requires natural gas, which adds to the carbon deficit.

. . . .

Refer to the following passage to answer the next nine questions.

Approximately one billion people worldwide have vitamin D deficiency. This deficiency is thought to be largely due to insufficient exposure to the sun. In some cases, poor diet can also play a role. There is increasing evidence that vitamin D deficiency also increases a person's susceptibility to autoimmune conditions. Additionally, a lack of vitamin D can impact bone development.

The main source of vitamin D in the body comes from exposing the skin to sunlight. Just 10 minutes of exposure to ultraviolet B radiation wavelengths between 280 and 315 nm, five days a week, will give most people enough vitamin D. However, extended exposure to ultraviolet radiation from the sun is known to increase the risk of skin cancer. Widespread campaigns for the use of sunscreen and sun avoidance have reduced the incidences of skin cancers. However, sunscreens with sun protection factors of 15 or higher also decrease the body's ability to synthesize vitamin D by 99%.

Radiation Type	UVA	UVB	UVC
Linked to	Aging	Burning	
Wavelength	400 nm to 315 nm	315 nm to 280 nm	280 nm to 100 nm
% reaching Earth at noon	0.95	0.05	0%—absorbed by ozone, molecular oxygen, and water vapor in the upper atmosphere
% reaching Earth before 10 A.M. & after 2 P.M.	0.99	0.01	0
% reaching Earth (average)	0.97	0.03	0

According to the information in the passage, what are the two consequences of vitamin D deficiency?

GED® TEST SCIENCE FLASH REVIEW

poor bone development and **autoimmune disease**

According to the passage, how do we make vitamin D?

. . . .

According to the passage, what type of radiation is necessary to make vitamin D?

. . . .

How much daily sunlight exposure is necessary to make vitamin D?

exposure to ultraviolet radiation

· ·

UVB radiation (315 to 280 nm)

· ·

10 minutes

From information in the passage, what are the apparent contradictions regarding vitamin D deficiency and sunlight exposure?

. . . .

When does the amount of UVA reaching Earth peak?

. . . .

When does the amount of UVB reaching Earth peak?

While exposure to ultraviolet radiation is important for your body to make vitamin D, it also puts you at risk for cancer.

· ·

Before 10 A.M. and after 2 P.M.

· ·

Noon

Does wearing sunscreen reduce UV exposure?

. . . .

Gathering the information in the passage and chart, explain in your own words how we can safely expose our skin to ultraviolet radiation to make vitamin D, but minimally risk skin cancer.

. . . .

Yes, when the SPF value is greater than 15.

· ·

Answers may vary.

A daily exposure of 10 minutes of UVB sunlight therapy at noon has been shown to reduce risks of autoimmune disease and improve bone health. UVB peaks at noon, while UVA peaks after 2 P.M. So, by going outside for 10 minutes around noon and wearing a sunscreen with an SPF factor less than 15, we can have beneficial sunlight therapy for vitamin D synthesis with a relatively low risk of skin cancer associated with exposure to ultraviolet radiation.

· ·

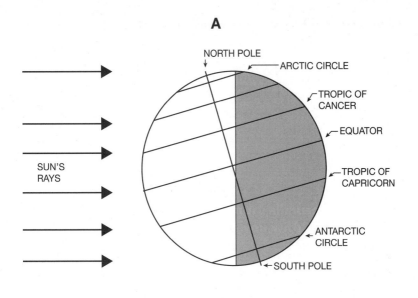

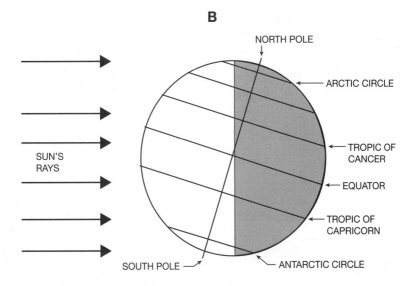

If you lived in New York, which diagram shows the Earth's position in June?

. . . .

In diagram **A**, New York is in summer and it is June.

GED® TEST SCIENCE FLASH REVIEW

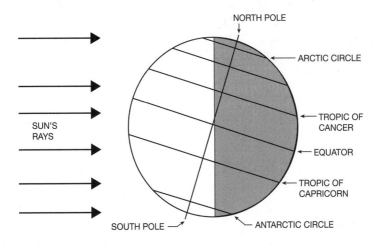

If you lived in the Antarctic Circle, what would the sun do at sunset every day?

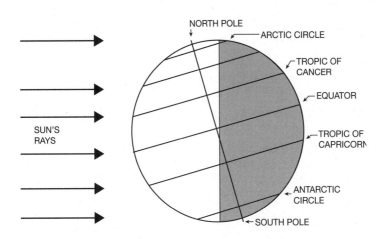

What is the season along the Tropic of Capricorn in this diagram?

Answers may vary.

The sun would not actually set, as this part of the planet is tilted so far toward the sun that there is no nighttime.

· ·

This season would be **winter**, because the days are shorter as that part of the earth is tilted away from the sun.

· ·

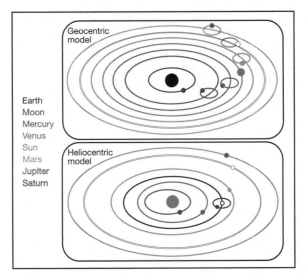

Geocentric model proposed by Ptolemy (top) and heliocentric model proposed by Copernicus (bottom)

One of these images is a heliocentric model of the solar system and the other is a geocentric model of the solar system.

What does a *heliocentric model* mean in the context of these images?

. . . .

A heliocentric model is set with the sun as the center of the solar system.

. . . .

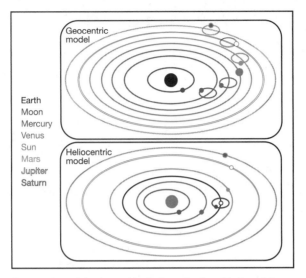

Earth
Moon
Mercury
Venus
Sun
Mars
Jupiter
Saturn

Geocentric model proposed by Ptolemy (top) and heliocentric model proposed by Copernicus (bottom)

One of these images is a heliocentric model of the solar system and the other is a geocentric model of the solar system.

What does a *geocentric model* mean in the context of these images?

. . . .

A geocentric model is set with Earth as the center of the solar system and universe.

· ·

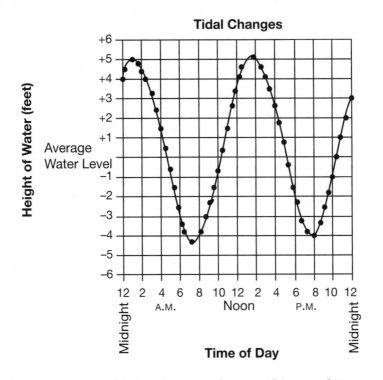

Tidal Changes

When is the next high tide according to this graph?

· ·

There will next be a high tide at 1 A.M.

· ·

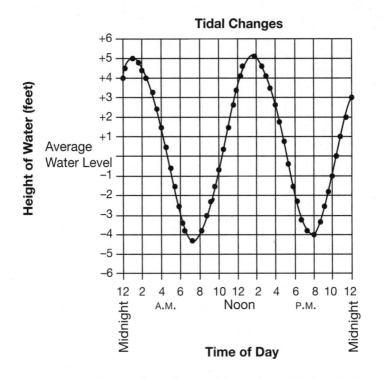

Tidal Changes

Height of Water (feet)

Average
Water Level

Time of Day

What can you determine about tides from this image?

· ·

They are cyclical, like waves.

· ·

Jovian planets are also known as gas giants. In the solar system, there are several of these planets, specifically Jupiter, Saturn, Neptune, and Uranus.

When considering these planets, what is different about them compared to Earth?
A. They are more dense and closer to the sun.
B. They are less dense and farther from the sun.
C. They are less dense and closer to the sun.
D. They are more dense and farther from the sun.

· ·

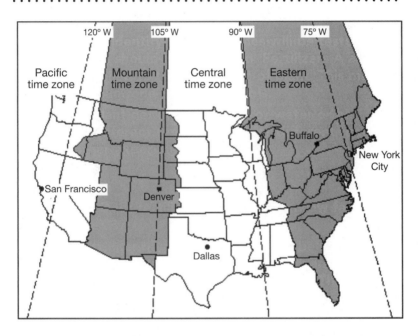

The time zone difference is about how many degrees per hour?

· ·

GED® TEST SCIENCE FLASH REVIEW

The correct answer is choice **B**, they are less dense and farther from the sun.

· ·

15 degrees per hour

· ·

Which celestial body is the largest?
A. Jupiter
B. Saturn
C. the Milky Way
D. the sun

. . . .

A _____ is a pattern or grouping of stars such as the Big Dipper.

. . . .

A _____ is a celestial body that has enough mass to be spherical, orbits the sun or other stars in other solar systems, and is not part of an asteroid belt.

Choice **C, the Milky Way**, is definitely the largest in size as it contains all the other celestial bodies listed.

· ·

A **constellation** is a pattern or grouping of stars such as the Big Dipper.

· ·

A **planet** is a celestial body that has enough mass to be spherical, orbits the sun or other stars in other solar systems, and is not part of an asteroid belt.

Why was Pluto reclassified as not a planet?

. . . .

When helium fuel runs out, the core of a star will expand and cool, and the upper layers will expand and eject material that will collect around the dying star to form a

_____.
A. black hole
B. red giant
C. planetary nebula
D. protostar

. . . .

Near the end of its life, the radius of a star increases to become a _____.
A. black hole
B. red giant
C. planetary nebula
D. protostar

Answers may vary.

Pluto was considered one of nine planets in Earth's solar system, but in the 1990s, astronomers learned that Pluto was not a planet in its own orbit, but part of a belt of asteroids.

. . . .

When helium fuel runs out, the core of a star will expand and cool, and the upper layers will expand and eject material that will collect around the dying star to form choice **C**, a **planetary nebula**.

. . . .

Near the end of its life, the radius of a star increases to become choice **B**, a **red giant**.

Some of the responses to oceanic acidification include reducing CO_2 emissions, climate engineering, iron fertilization, and using carbon-negative fuels. Which of these is a practice that is already being done?

. . . .

Earth's inner core is a solid mass of iron with a temperature of about 7,000°F. The high heat at Earth's core is a combination of which three of the following factors?
- residual heat from the moon's formation
- residual heat from Earth's formation
- frictional heating, caused by the tectonic plates moving against each other
- frictional heating, caused by denser parts of the core moving toward the center
- decay of radioactive elements, such as uranium, in the core. The inner core is approximately 1,500 miles in diameter.

. . . .

Which of the following is NOT part of the rocky mantle?
- silicon
- oxygen
- magnesium
- iron
- aluminum
- calcium
- meteors
- water

reducing CO$_2$ emissions

In a statement from 2009, the InterAcademy Panel recommended that global anthropogenic CO$_2$ be reduced to 50% of the 1990 level by 2050.

· ·

- residual heat from Earth's formation
- frictional heating, caused by denser parts of the core moving toward the center
- Decay of radioactive elements, such as uranium, in the core. The inner core is approximately 1,500 miles in diameter.

· ·

At this time, **meteors** are not a part of the rocky mantle.

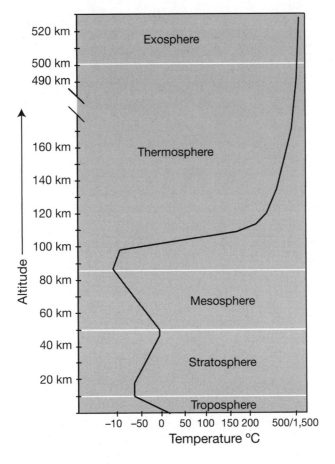

The troposphere is the lowest portion of Earth's atmosphere. What percentages of the atmosphere's mass, water vapor, and aerosols do you think it contains, respectively?

A. 50%, 32%, 40%

B. 70%, 60%, 77%

C. 80%, 99%, 99%

D. 75%, 65%, 65%

The correct answer is choice **C, 80%, 99%, 99%**. The troposphere contains 80% of the atmosphere's mass and 99% of the water vapor and aerosols.

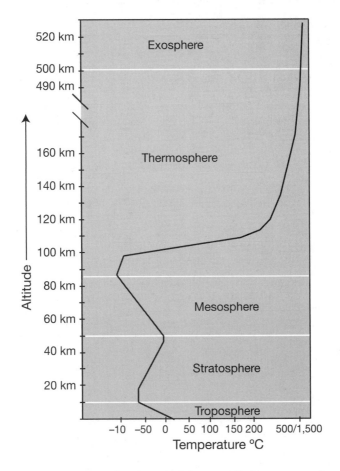

The stratosphere is the second layer of the atmosphere and is known for having stratified layers of temperature. How far up is this layer?

. . . .

Carbon is found in which of the following items?
A. oceans, in the form of bicarbonate ions (HCO_3^-)
B. living organisms
C. fossil fuels such as coal, oil, and natural gas
D. all the above

. . . .

This layer exists anywhere from 10 km to 50 km up.

· ·

Choice **D**, all the items contain carbon.

· ·

Since the Industrial Revolution, when the consumption of energy to power machinery began to substantially expand, people have increased the concentration of carbon dioxide in the atmosphere by ___ by burning fossil fuels and cutting down forests that reduce the concentration of carbon dioxide.

A. 10%
B. 50%
C. 30%
D. 80%

. . . .

Burning fossil fuels and forests also releases nitrogen. All forms of fixed nitrogen are greenhouse gases that cause global warming.

What can you conclude from this pair of statements?

. . . .

Earth's upper mantle is rigid and, together with the crust, is part of the lithosphere. The lower mantle flows slowly at a rate of _____ per year.

A. a foot
B. a few centimeters
C. a mile
D. a kilometer

Since the Industrial Revolution, when the consumption of energy to power machinery began to substantially expand, people have increased the concentration of carbon dioxide in the atmosphere by choice **C, 30%** by burning fossil fuels and cutting down forests that reduce the concentration of carbon dioxide.

· ·

Answers may vary.

Burning fossil fuels and forests causes global warming.

· ·

The lower mantle flows slowly at a rate of choice **B, a few centimeters** per year.

Evidence suggests that about 200 million years ago, all continents were a part of one landmass, now called _____.

. . . .

Over the years, the continents have slowly separated in a process called _____.

. . . .

The force needed to move billions of tons of rock is great. When plates move, some of the energy is released as _____.

Evidence suggests that about 200 million years ago, all continents were a part of one landmass, now called **Pangaea**.

. . . .

Over the years, the continents have slowly separated in a process called **continental drift**.

. . . .

The force needed to move billions of tons of rock is great. When plates move, some of the energy is released as **earthquakes**.

When two tectonic plates separate, energy is released, earthquakes occur, and magma is released. The Atlantic Ocean was formed by the separation of plates over millions of years.

What is the word for this type of movement by the tectonic plates?
- subduction
- diverging
- converging

. . . .

At some tectonic plate boundaries, one plate slides under the other. As the plate slides under the other, the crust melts as it goes deeper into the earth. What is this process called?
- subduction
- diverging
- converging

. . . .

As one plate slides under the other, the crust melts as it goes deeper into the earth. This creates _____, which rises to the surface and can form volcanoes.

To diverge is to separate, so when two plates separate, this is called **diverging**.

· ·

Subduction is what happens when one plate slides under the other.

· ·

This creates **magma**, which rises to the surface and can form volcanoes.

Select the best answer to fill the blank from the choices that follow.

_____ plates result in the creation of mountains. For example, the Andes Mountains were formed by the Nazca Plate being pushed into the South American Plate. When two oceanic plates meet each other, it often results in the formation of an island arc system.

• Subducting
• Diverging
• Converging

· ·

Molten material from inside Earth often breaks through the floor of the ocean and flows from fissures, where it is cooled by water, resulting in the formation of _____.

· ·

As molten material flows from a fissure, it forms adjacent _____.

Converging plates result in the creation of mountains.

· ·

Molten material from inside Earth often breaks through the floor of the ocean and flows from fissures, where it is cooled by water, resulting in the formation of **igneous rocks**.

· ·

As molten material flows from a fissure, it forms adjacent **ridges**.

GED® TEST SCIENCE FLASH REVIEW

Wind currents are generally measured in meters per second, also known as what?

. . . .

If a wind current is moving at 25 knots, how many miles per hour would that be?
(1 knot = 1.15 mph)

. . . .

The Gulf Stream is an ocean current that runs up from the tip of Florida, flowing along the eastern coastline of the United States to Newfoundland, before crossing the Atlantic Ocean. Because of this warm water being carried, what can you determine about the Gulf Stream's effect?

knots

(1 knot = 1.15 miles per hour or 1.85 kilometers per hour)

· ·

28.75 miles per hour

· ·

Answers may vary.

Because it carries warm water, the Gulf Stream makes Northern Europe warmer than it would be without it.

What is one effect of El Niño on the global weather?

. . . .

The effects of human activity on the planet's plant and animal _____ are a growing concern of environmental activists and scientists.

. . . .

During the last 100 years, temperatures have increased by ___°C.

Answers may vary.

- increased rainfall across the eastern Pacific Ocean
- reduces the upwelling of cold, nutrient-rich water that sustains large fish populations along the west coast of South America
- worldwide temperature shifts
- higher temperatures in western Canada and the upper plains of the United States
- colder temperatures in the southern United States
- Parts of the southern and eastern coast of Africa can experience severe drought.

· ·

The effects of human activity on **biodiversity** are a growing concern of environmental activists and scientists.

· ·

In the last 100 years, temperatures have increased by **1°C**.

Increased levels of carbon dioxide and other greenhouse gases cause increased temperatures worldwide known as _____.

. . . .

The sun's energy reaches Earth in the form of light radiation. Plants use this light to synthesize sugar molecules, which people consume and derive energy from. What is this process called?

. . . .

The sun heats Earth's surface and drives _____ within the atmosphere and oceans, producing winds and ocean currents.

Increased levels of carbon dioxide and other greenhouse gases cause increased temperatures worldwide known as **global warming**.

. . . .

photosynthesis

. . . .

The sun heats Earth's surface and drives **convection** within the atmosphere and oceans, producing winds and ocean currents.

_____ refers to the conversion of solar energy to another, more useful form.

. . . .

What is the equator?

. . . .

What is the geochemical cycle?

Solar power refers to the conversion of solar energy to another, more useful form.

. . . .

The equator is the imaginary line drawn around the earth that runs east and west at 0° latitude.

. . . .

The geochemical cycle is the circulation of elements in the biosphere. For example, water, carbon, and nitrogen are recycled in the biosphere. A water molecule in the cell of your eye could have been at some point in the ocean, in the atmosphere, in a leaf of a tree, or in the cell of a bear's foot.

What is geology?

. . . .

What is a hemisphere?

. . . .

What is igneous rock?

Geology is the study of rocks and minerals.

. . . .

A hemisphere is half of the earth, either the northern or southern half of the globe as divided by the equator or the eastern or western half as divided by the prime meridian.

. . . .

An igneous rock is a rock formed through the cooling of magma.

What is a land breeze?

. . . .

What is latitude?

. . . .

What is longitude?

A land breeze develops on the shoreline due to unequal heating of the air above the land and ocean. Land breeze occurs at night when the air above the land is cooler and the air above the ocean is warmer. The breeze blows from the land to the sea.

• •

Latitude is the coordinate used to measure positions on Earth north or south of Earth's equator, ranging from 0° at the equator to 90° at the poles. Latitude is measured in degrees, minutes, and seconds.

• •

Longitude is the coordinate used to measure positions on Earth east or west of the prime meridian, ranging from 0° at the prime meridian to 180° east or 180° west longitude. The prime meridian goes through Greenwich, England. Longitude is measured in degrees, minutes, and seconds.

What is a longitudinal wave?

· ·

What is retrograde motion?

· ·

What is right ascension?

A longitudinal wave has the same direction of vibration as its direction of travel. The motion of the particles in the medium is parallel to the direction of wave propagation. Sound is an example of a longitudinal wave.

· ·

Retrograde motion is the apparent westward motion of objects in the sky from one night to another.

· ·

Right ascension is the celestial coordinate similar to that of longitude on Earth. Right ascension is measured in hours, minutes, and seconds with 24 hours making up 360° around the celestial sphere.

What is a rock cycle?

. . . .

What is a sea breeze?

. . . .

What is the temperate zone?

A rock cycle is a concept in geology that summarizes how rocks of different types are formed and how they can be transformed from one type into another.

. . . .

A sea breeze develops on the shoreline due to unequal heating of the air above the land and ocean. Sea breeze occurs during the day when the air above the ocean is cooler and the air above the land is warmer. The breeze blows from the sea to the land.

. . . .

The temperate zone is a climatic zone characterized by four seasons, usually a hot summer, cold winter, and moderate spring and fall.

What is a terrestrial planet?

. . . .

What is a terminal moraine?

. . . .

What is the polar zone?

A terrestrial planet is one of the inner planets of the solar system that have characteristics similar to those of Earth. The terrestrial planets are Mercury, Venus, Earth, and Mars. They are small, have few or no moons, and have no rings. They have thin or no atmosphere, are rocky, and have high density and low mass. Terrestrial planets are located close to the sun and are close to each other. They have long rotation rates and have short revolution periods around the sun.

. . . .

A terminal moraine is a ridge of material deposited by a glacier at its farthest point of advance.

. . . .

The polar zone is the climatic zone near the North or South Pole characterized by long, cold winters and short, cool summers.

Match the part of the cell with its description:

1. nucleus	A. cell parts found only in plant cells
2. mitochondria	B. the element that controls the transfer of material into and out of the cell
3. ribosomes	
	C. where the DNA of a cell is found
4. plasma membrane	
	D. cell parts found only in animal cells
5. centrioles	
	E. the site of the cell where substances break down to obtain energy
6. vacuoles	
	F. the part of the cell where the synthesis of protein takes place

. . . .

Answer the following question using a Punnett square.

Angelfish exist in a number of different colorations. Black angelfish have the genotype (DD), indicating that the black gene is dominant. If you breed a black angelfish (DD) with an angelfish with a recessive gold (gg) genotype, what will result?

Note: A Dg genotype will result in a hybrid genotype and produce a hybrid black angelfish that has a milky black coloration.
Black: ___%
Hybrid black: ___%
Gold: ___%

. . . .

A puppy has its mother's brown eyes. The puppy's eye color is an example of _____.

1.—**C.** The nucleus is where the DNA of a cell is found.

2.—**E.** The mitochondria is the site of the cell where substances break down to obtain energy.

3.—**F.** Ribosomes are the part of the cell where the synthesis of protein takes place.

4.—**B.** The plasma membrane is the element that controls the transfer of material into and out of the cell.

5.—**D.** Centrioles are cell parts found only in animal cells.

6.—**A.** Vacuoles are cell parts found only in plant cells.

· ·

Black: **0%**

Hybrid black: 100%

Gold: **0%**

Black angelfish

		D	D
Gold angelfish	g	Dg	Dg
	g	Dg	Dg

The Punnett square shows that when crossing a black angelfish that has dominant black genes (DD) with an angelfish that has recessive gold genes (gg), all the offspring (100%) will be hybrid (Dg).

· ·

The puppy's eye color is an example of **phenotype**. Phenotype is the physical or behavioral expression of a gene (for example, eye color, hair color, and so on).

Yellow (r) is a recessive allele in plants. Red is dominant (R). Complete this Punnett square for a homozygous yellow plant crossed with a heterozygous red plant.

PLANT (Rr)

	R	r
PLANT (rr) r		
r		

· ·

With yellow (r) as a recessive allele in plants and red as a dominant (R), what would the percentage of each type be if a homozygous yellow plant is crossed with a heterozygous red plant?

____% of the offspring would be homozygous yellow (rr)
____% of the offspring would be heterozygous red (Rr)
____% of the offspring would be homozygous red (RR)

· ·

Yellow (r) is a recessive allele in plants. Red is dominant (R). Complete this Punnett square to show what would result if two heterozygous red plants were bred.

PLANT (Rr)

	R	r
PLANT (Rr) R		
r		

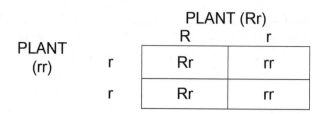

                    PLANT (Rr)
                    R   r

PLANT
(rr)   r | Rr | rr |
            r | Rr | rr |

....

50% of the offspring would be homozygous yellow (rr)

50% of the offspring would be heterozygous red (Rr)

0% of the offspring would be homozygous red (RR)

....

                    PLANT (Rr)
                    R   r

PLANT
(Rr)   r | RR | Rr |
            r | Rr | rr |

With yellow (r) as a recessive allele in plants and red as a dominant (R), what would the percentage of each of the following types be based on the crossing of two heterozygous plants?

____% of the offspring would be homozygous yellow (rr)

____% of the offspring would be heterozygous red (Rr)

____% of the offspring would be homozygous red (RR)

· ·

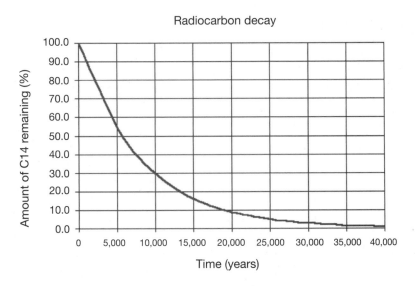

Radiocarbon decay

After 10,000 years ___% of the C14 sample remains.

· ·

25% of the offspring would be homozygous yellow (rr)

50% of the offspring would be heterozygous red (Rr)

25% of the offspring would be homozygous red (RR)

. . . .

After 10,000 years **30%** of the sample remains.

. . . .

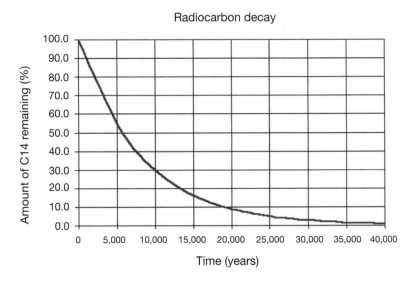

Radiocarbon decay

After 20,000 years ___% of the sample remains.

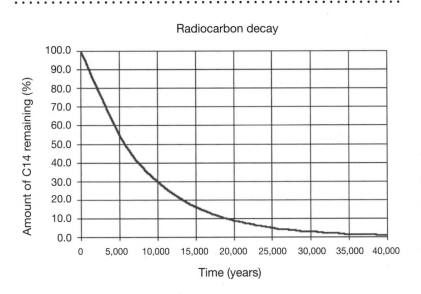

Radiocarbon decay

After 25,000 years ___% of the sample remains.

After 20,000 years **10%** of the sample remains.

. . . .

After 25,000 years **5%** of the sample remains.

. . . .

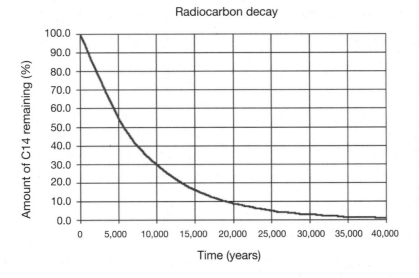

Radiocarbon decay

A scientist finds a fossilized bone that has about 25% of the natural amount of the C14 remaining. Using the chart, what is the approximate age of the bone?

. . . .

Which of the following statements explains how biogeography is evidence for evolution?
A. Offspring carry the traits of both parents.
B. Different species are not likely to interbreed.
C. The fossil record shows the sequence of evolution in layers of sediment.
D. Neighboring species in different habitats often can share a common ancestor.

. . . .

The bone is roughly **12,500** years old.

· ·

Choice **D** explains how one species can diverge into two species over time when divided into two separate habitats. A classic example of this is the case of finches on the Galapagos Islands, where finch species diverged from a common ancestor to adapt to the unique habitats of each island.

· ·

The peppered moth lives in the in the United Kingdom and has both light and dark variations. During the Industrial Revolution (1760–1840), many of the trees on which the moths lived became covered with dark soot. Over a period of just 50 years, the population of peppered moths in Manchester, England, changed so that dark moths made up almost the entire population. After the Clean Air Act of 1956, the air quality changed and dark moths became rare. This is an example of _____.

• •

Speciation provides evidence for the theory of _____.

• •

The body systems work together to stay in equilibrium or homeostasis. Which of the following is an example of the body trying to maintain homeostasis?
A. weight gain
B. bruising
C. digestion
D. shivering

This is an example of **natural selection**.

According to natural selection, whether a given trait is advantageous depends on the environment of the organism. In this case, the moths that were better camouflaged (those that were the color of the soot-covered trees) survived and reproduced.

· ·

Speciation provides evidence for the theory of **evolution**. Evolution is the gradual change of inherited characteristics in a population over time.

· ·

Choice **D**, **shivering**, is an example of the body trying to maintain homeostasis. The body systems work with one another to maintain a state of balance or homeostasis (functioning within a normal range). For example, shivering ("goose bumps") and sweating are your body's response to being too cold or too hot. Your skin and spinal cord sense cold and send signals to the muscles to contract and shiver. In contrast, as your temperature rises the blood vessels in your skin get larger, called vasodilation, which allows for cooling of the blood. Sweat glands are activated when you are hot in an attempt to cool the body and return to homeostasis.

From a nutritional perspective, list four problem areas with this burger.

Deluxe Fast Food Burger

Nutrition Facts

Serving Size 216 g

Amount per Serving

Calories 615   Calories from fat 333 calories

% Daily Value*

Total fat 37 g	57%
Saturated fat 12 g	60%
Cholesterol 88 mg	29%
Sodium 1,090 mg	46%
Total carbohydrate 48 g	16%
Dietary fiber 3 g	12%
Sugars 8 g	
Protein 26 g	

Vitamin A	6%	Vitamin C	6%
Calcium	30%	Iron	25%

*Percent Daily Values are based on a 2,000-calorie diet. Your daily values may be higher or lower depending on your calorie needs.

Answers will vary.

This burger is high in calories, high in total fat, high in saturated fat, high in cholesterol, and high in sodium, and more than 50% of its calories are from fat.

Consider that the recommended daily intake for a 30-year-old woman is about 1,800 calories. From a nutritional perspective, list at least two health complications that could result from regularly eating food with nutritional content like this burger.

Deluxe Fast Food Burger

Nutrition Facts

Serving Size 216 g

Amount per Serving

Calories 615	Calories from fat 333 calories

	% Daily Value*
Total fat 37 g	57%
Saturated fat 12 g	60%
Cholesterol 88 mg	29%
Sodium 1,090 mg	46%
Total carbohydrate 48 g	16%
Dietary fiber 3 g	12%
Sugars 8 g	
Protein 26 g	

Vitamin A	6%	•	Vitamin C	6%
Calcium	30%	•	Iron	25%

*Percent Daily Values are based on a 2,000-calorie diet. Your daily values may be higher or lower depending on your calorie needs.

Answers will vary.

The problems that can result from a diet that contains many similar items are weight gain, heart disease, obesity, high blood pressure, and diabetes.

Match each of the functions with its correct system.

1. movement	A. nervous
2. breathing	B. endocrine
3. metabolism	C. circulatory
4. homeostasis	D. musculoskeletal
5. blood flow	E. digestive
6. hormone regulation	F. respiratory

. . . .

List the following parts from simple units to complex:
- **organ**
- **tissue**
- **cell**
- **body system**

. . . .

Which of the following is an example of the body trying to maintain homeostasis?
- **bleeding**
- **thinking**
- **sweating**
- **digestion**
- **crying**
- **dreaming**

1.—**D.** Movement is a function of the musculoskeletal system.

2.—**F.** Breathing is a function of the respiratory system.

3.—**E.** Metabolism is a function of the digestive system.

4.—**A.** Homeostasis is a function of the nervous system.

5.—**C.** Blood flow is a function of the circulatory system.

6.—**B.** Hormone regulation is a function of the endocrine system.

. . . .

1. cell

2. tissue

3. organ

4. body system

Cells are the smallest and simplest unit in an organism. Tissues are made up of cells (for example, muscle tissue is made of muscle cells). Organs are made of tissues (a heart is made of heart tissue), and finally, organs are organized into body systems (for example, the nervous system, the digestive system, and so on).

. . . .

Sweating is an example of the body trying to maintain homeostasis through evaporative cooling.

African oxpeckers feed on the insects that are on the backs of zebras and other large African animals. This is an example of which of the following symbiotic relationships?
- parasitism
- mutualism
- commensalism

. . . .

Lice feed on the skin and blood of the host. This is an example of which of the following symbiotic relationships?
- parasitism
- mutualism
- commensalism

. . . .

Some spiders build their webs on blades of grass. This is an example of which of the following symbiotic relationships?
- parasitism
- mutualism
- commensalism

This is an example of **mutualism**. Both oxpeckers and the zebras are benefiting, which describes a mutualistic relationship. Parasitism describes a relationship between two organisms where one benefits at the expense of the other. Commensalism describes a benefit for one organism and no harm or benefit to the other.

. . . .

This is an example of **parasitism**. Lice are benefiting, and the hosts are being deprived of blood and skin, clearly a parasitic relationship. Parasitism describes a relationship between two organisms where one benefits at the expense of the other. Commensalism describes a benefit for one organism and no harm or benefit to the other. Mutualism describes a relationship between two organisms where both organisms benefit.

. . . .

This is an example of **commensalism**. The spiders are using the grass as a place to build their webs, but there is no impact on the grass, positive or negative. Commensalism describes a benefit for one organism and no harm or benefit to the other. Parasitism describes a relationship between two organisms where one benefits at the expense of the other. Mutualism describes a relationship between two organisms where both organisms benefit.

The pea crab lives in the mantle cavity of mollusks, oysters, sea urchins, or sand dollars, using the host for oxygen, protection, and a source of food. These tiny crabs ingest food that is part of the host's diet and often may feed on the mucous strings that help carry the food to the host's mouth, damaging them. This is an example of _____.

- parasitism
- commensalism
- mutualism

. . . .

Gymnosporangium is a genus of fungus that first grows on juniper trees and has its spores grow on fruit trees. As those spores grow on the fruit trees, they cause a loss in fruit production, damaging the reproduction of the trees. This is an example of _____.

- parasitism
- commensalism
- mutualism

. . . .

Schistosoma is a genus of fluke or flatworm commonly known as a blood fluke. This flatworm lives within the blood vessels of humans and is the major cause of a group of infections known as schistosomiasis, which can lead to internal organ damage and infertility. This is an example of _____.

- parasitism
- commensalism
- mutualism

This is an example of **parasitism**.

· ·

This is an example of **parasitism**.

· ·

This is an example of **parasitism**.

The Mountain Alcon Blue butterfly larvae release chemicals that confuse *Myrmica schencki* ants into believing that those larvae are queen ant larvae. The ants then bring the butterfly larvae into the ant brood and feed the butterflies preferentially over their own larvae as they think they will turn out to be queen ants. This is an example of _____.

- parasitism
- commensalism
- mutualism

. . . .

The energy available in an ecosystem is greatest at which level?

A. producer
B. primary consumer
C. secondary consumer
D. tertiary consumer

. . . .

Of the following options, in what way do humans contribute to desertification most?

A. drought
B. overgrazing
C. acid rain
D. overhunting

This is an example of **parasitism**.

．．

The energy available in an ecosystem is greatest at choice **A**, the **producer** level. The energy available is greatest at the bottom of the energy pyramid (producer) and decreases as you move up the pyramid and the population numbers decrease. Plants are producers. Secondary consumers feed on primary consumers and are carnivores or omnivores. Humans are tertiary consumers because we consume primary and secondary consumers.

．．

Humans contribute to desertification most by choice **B**, **overgrazing**. Desertification occurs when an already dry land area becomes increasingly arid and dry. It is less able to support plants and animals. Humans contribute to desertification of ecosystems through deforestation (often using trees and other plant material for fuel or for construction materials), overgrazing, and poor farming practices; therefore this choice is the correct answer. Drought is a natural occurrence and does not (in and of itself) cause desertification unless it occurs in the extreme. Acid rain does not contribute to drought. Overhunting can result in damage to the ecosystem, but is not the best answer.

Harmful algal blooms are naturally occurring events, but they appear to be increasing in intensity and frequency. Blooms occur when environmental conditions change to be more favorable to increased algae growth. Nutrients such as phosphates (phosphorus) and nitrogen (found in fertilizer and animal waste products) encourage the growth of algae.

What are some human practices that could be contributing to the increase in harmful algal blooms?

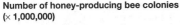

Number of honey-producing bee colonies (× 1,000,000)

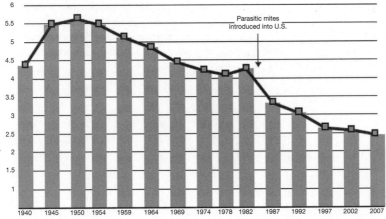

Data source: U.S. Department of Agriculture's (USDA) National Agricultural Statistics Service (NASS). NB: Data collected for producers with five or more colonies. Honey producing colonies are the maximum number of colonies from which honey was taken during the year. It is possible to take honey from colonies that did not survive the entire year.

Which of the following conclusions can be supported by the graph?
A. Parasitic mites caused the decline in bee populations.
B. Bee populations will become extinct because of parasitic mites.
C. Parasitic mites may have contributed to a decline in bee populations.
D. Bee populations increased until the introduction of parasitic mites.

Answer will vary. Here is an example.

Since algae like nitrates and phosphates, which are found in fertilizer and animal waste products, farming practices and fertilizer use can be contributing to increases in algae blooms. Runoff from farms (especially animal farms) near waterways or watersheds can result in wastes and fertilizers flowing into the ocean and other bodies of water during storms. Similar results can occur with fertilizer use.

. . . .

The correct answer is choice **C**. The introduction of parasitic mites is not the only cause; however, it may have contributed to the decline in bee populations. Bee populations were in decline prior to the introduction of mites in 1983. Although there is a downward trend in bee populations, there is no way to conclude that bees will become extinct. Bee populations were decreasing before mites were introduced.

Tapeworms are segmented flatworms that attach themselves to the insides of the intestines of host animals such as cows, pigs, and humans. They survive by eating the host's partly digested food, depriving the host of nutrients.

This is an example of which kind of relationship?

. . . .

The plasma membrane of a cell regulates transport of materials. Osmosis occurs when molecules inside a cell are highly concentrated and are forced to move through the membrane to an area of lower concentration. What is the word for this pressure that pushes these molecules?

. . . .

When osmosis occurs in a cell, where molecules move from where they are highly concentrated through the cell membrane to where they are less concentrated, what is the word for these concentration levels being the same?

This is an example of **parasitism**. A parasite species benefits at the expense of another species.

· ·

This is called **osmotic pressure**. If the word *osmosis* is in the description, it is possible to see the relationship with the word *osmotic*. This type of pressure forces osmosis to happen.

· ·

The word for the same concentration of molecules on both sides of a cell membrane is **equilibrium**.

In the diagram, in what direction would the sugar molecules move in this container through osmosis?

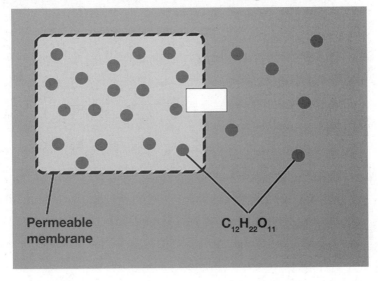

Permeable membrane

$C_{12}H_{22}O_{11}$

. . . .

Of the items listed here, which are specific to a plant cell?
- nucleus
- chloroplast
- cytoplasm
- cell wall
- mitochondria
- ribosomes
- vacuoles

. . . .

Cells in a multicellular organism have specific purposes. Blood is composed of plasma as well as red and white blood cells. One of these cells carries oxygen throughout the body, and the other fights pathogens as a part of the body's immune system. Which does which?

The sugar molecules would move **to the right** in order to achieve equilibrium, as can be seen in the following illustration.

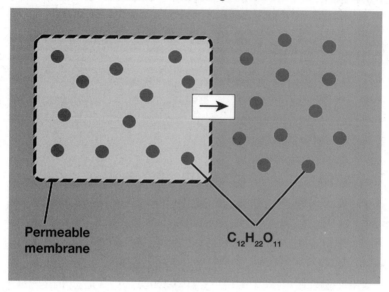

Permeable membrane

$C_{12}H_{22}O_{11}$

. . . .

Chloroplast, cell wall, and **vacuoles** are all specific to plant cells. The rest are all common to both animal and plant cells.

. . . .

Red blood cells carry oxygen and white blood cells fight pathogens.

What is the Golgi complex?

· ·

Which of the following parts of a cell contains enzymes that help with intracellular digestion?
• **Golgi complex**
• **endoplasmic reticulum**
• **lysosomes**
• **cytoplasm**
• **mitochondria**
• **nucleolus**

· ·

The *genotype* of an organism affects the *phenotype* of that same organism. Is each item in the list a genotype or a phenotype?
• **recessive eye color genes**
• **blue eyes**
• **sex determination**
• **female**
• **curling tongue**
• **dominant hair color genes**

The **Golgi complex** is a series of small sacs that synthesizes, packages, and secretes cellular products to the plasma membrane. Its function is directing the transport of material within the cell and exporting material out of the cell.

. . . .

Lysosomes contain enzymes that help with intracellular digestion. Lysosomes have a large presence in cells that actively engage in phagocytosis—the process by which cells consume large particles of food. White blood cells that often engulf and digest bacteria and cellular debris are abundant in lysosomes.

. . . .

recessive eye color genes—genotype

blue eyes—phenotype

sex determination—genotype

female—phenotype

curling tongue—phenotype

dominant hair color genes—genotype

Mitosis and meiosis are both forms of cellular reproduction. *Mitosis* is the splitting of a cell into two with all the same genetic information being reproduced in both new cells. *Meiosis* involves splitting of a cell and combining with another cell, with the genetic information being split in half and combined with the other cell.
Is each process in this list an example of mitosis or meiosis?
* skin regeneration
* blood production
* pollen production
* growth of a multicellular organism
* egg cell production

. . . .

The genotype of an organism affects the phenotype of that same organism. A Punnett square can be used to represent the possible _____ that offspring of parents with known _____ could have.

. . . .

Human males have an X and a Y chromosome while human females have two X chromosomes. Since meiosis involves splitting up the genetic information in the sex cells, do the male's or the female's chromosomes determine the sex of a human offspring?

skin regeneration—mitosis

blood production—mitosis

pollen production—meiosis

growth of a multicellular organism—mitosis

egg cell production—meiosis

· ·

A Punnett square can be used to represent the possible **phenotypes** that offspring of parents with known **genotypes** could have.

· ·

The sex chromosome supplied by the **male** determines the sex of the human offspring.

In birds, males have a matched pair of sex chromosomes (WW), while females have an unmatched pair (WZ). In this case, do the male's or the female's chromosomes determine the sex of the bird offspring?

· ·

Twins occur when either a fertilized cell splits or when two different egg cells are fertilized by two different sperm cells. If the twins are a boy and a girl, which of these happened?

· ·

Genetic mutations are usually harmful or do not directly affect the organism, but there are sometimes beneficial mutations. Here are some mutations. Is each of the following harmful or beneficial?
• white fur on polar bears
• cystic fibrosis
• lactose tolerance in humans
• antibiotic resistance in bacteria
• sickle cell anemia
• cancer

In birds, the sex chromosome supplied by the **female** determines the sex of offspring.

· ·

These are fraternal twins, so two different egg cells were fertilized by two different sperm cells.

· ·

white fur on polar bears—beneficial

cystic fibrosis—harmful

lactose tolerance in humans—beneficial

antibiotic resistance in bacteria—beneficial for the bacteria

sickle cell anemia—harmful

cancer—harmful

What is the term for how life developed on Earth?

. . . .

Fossils are often located in sedimentary rocks, which form during compression of settling mud, debris, and sand. The order of layers of sedimentary rock shows the sequence in which life on Earth evolved. In what sequence would the fossils listed here appear?
- fish
- mammals
- single-celled organisms
- multicellular organisms
- amphibians
- reptiles
- birds

. . . .

Fill in the blank with the correct term.

An _____ is an organism that requires an oxygen source for survival and growth.

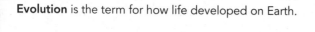

Evolution is the term for how life developed on Earth.

. . . .

single-celled organisms → multicellular organisms → fish → amphibians → reptiles → birds → mammals

The simplest organisms are in the bottom layer, while top layers contain increasingly complex and modern organisms in a pattern that suggests evolution.

. . . .

Answer: An **aerobe** is an organism that requires an oxygen source for survival and growth.

Which of the following is artificial selection and which is natural selection?
- Wild mustard becoming broccoli, cauliflower, kale, and cabbage
- A polyphemus moth with eye-shaped spots on its wings

. . . .

Match each of the body parts with its correct system.

1. tendon   A. nervous system

2. spinal cord   B. circulatory system

3. lymph nodes   C. digestive system

4. larynx   D. musculoskeletal system

5. gallbladder   E. respiratory system

6. thymus   F. endocrine system

. . . .

Messages are sent from parts of the body to other parts through the nervous system. What is an example of such a message?

Wild mustard becoming broccoli, cauliflower, kale, and cabbage is **artificial selection**, as farmers bred and manipulated the wild mustard plant into becoming these various other common vegetables.

A polyphemus moth with eye-shaped spots on its wings is **natural selection**, as this was a mutation that led to the survival of the moths with those spots, as they kept predators from eating the moths.

. . . .

1.—**D.** The tendon is a part of the musculoskeletal system.

2.—**A.** The spinal cord is a part of the nervous system.

3.—**B.** The lymph nodes are a part of the circulatory system.

4.—**E.** The larynx is a part of the respiratory system.

5.—**C.** The gallbladder is a part of the digestive system.

6.—**F.** The thymus is a part of the endocrine system.

. . . .

Your answer may vary.

Any input from a sensory organ like the nose, eyes, skin, ears, and tongue is transmitted through the nervous system. For example, if eyes see an apple, that message goes through the nervous system to the brain, which then sends information to other parts of your body, such as to the digestive system to prepare to digest the apple.

As your temperature rises, the blood vessels in your skin get larger. This process, called *vasodilation*, allows for cooling of the blood. What is the purpose of this cooling of the blood?
- circulation
- digestion
- homeostasis

. . . .

List at least three general parts of the body that are included in the musculoskeletal system.

. . . .

Which of the following is true about osmosis?
A. Water will move across a semi-permeable membrane from an area of high solute concentration to an area of low concentration.
B. Water does not move across semi-permeable membranes.
C. Water moves across a semi-permeable membrane driven by a difference in the amounts of solute on the two sides of the membrane until equilibrium is reached.
D. A semi-permeable membrane allows large particles to move across with the help of water molecules.

The correct answer is **homeostasis**, which is how the body systems work with one another to maintain a state of balance.

. . . .

Answers will vary.

Muscles, **ligaments**, **tendons**, **bones**, and **cartilage** are all part of the musculoskeletal system.

. . . .

The correct answer is choice **C**. Osmotic pressure forces highly concentrated molecules to move across a membrane into areas of lower concentration until a balance in reached. This balance is called equilibrium. The other choices are incorrect because the first option is the opposite of what actually occurs, water does move across semi-permeable membranes, and a semi-permeable membrane allows only small particles to move across.

Cells are the building blocks of life. Which of the following is NOT true about cells?
A. Only some cells contain genetic material.
B. Given the right conditions, cells will remain alive outside of the body.
C. Cells respond to their environments.
D. All cells contain a membrane that controls which molecules enter the cell.

. . . .

The graph shows the population of rabbits in one particular area. What is the carrying capacity of the rabbit population?

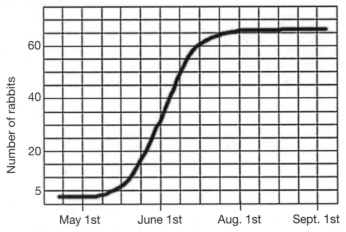

. . . .

Some plants have fungus colonies that live on their roots. The plants provide carbohydrates to the fungus in return primarily for phosphate and nitrogenous compounds. This is an example of:
A. mutualism
B. predation
C. commensalism
D. parasitism

All cells contain genetic material, so choice **A** is NOT true.

. . . .

The carrying capacity is **65**, because this is where the population levels out after increasing steadily. The reproductive ability of the population is limited by the available resources. Under ideal conditions, with ample food and space and no predators, all living organisms have the capacity to reproduce infinitely. However, resources are limited, limiting the population of a species. This is called carrying capacity of the population. The carrying capacity of a population is the maximum population size that the environment can sustain given the necessary resources (food, habitat, water) available in the environment.

. . . .

The correct answer is choice **A**, **mutualism**, which is the type of symbiotic relationship in which both organisms benefit. This is not a predatory relationship in which one organism captures and feeds on another. Commensalism is symbiosis in which one organism benefits and the other is neither harmed nor rewarded, but here the fungus as well as the plants are benefiting from this relationship. In a parasitic relationship, one organism benefits at the expense of the other.

Tay-Sachs disease is a rare genetic disorder that impacts muscle coordination and cognition starting at 6 months of age and typically results in death at an early age. The allele for Tay-Sachs disease is recessive.

Complete the Punnett square for two parents who are carriers of the gene (Tt).

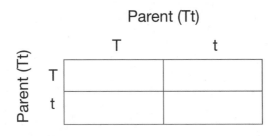

Parent (Tt)

. . . .

Based on a Punnett square for carriers of a Tay-Sachs disease gene (Tt), what is the likelihood that the children of two heterozygous parents will carry the gene for Tay-Sachs disease (homozygous or heterozygous)?

TT: _____%
Tt: _____%
tt: _____%

. . . .

Which of the following statements is NOT true about the endocrine system?
A. Diabetes is a disease that affects the production of glucose-regulating insulin in the endocrine system.
B. It works toward homeostasis in the body.
C. It includes the pituitary, thyroid, thymus, and pancreas.
D. Glands in the endocrine system send out chemical messages via hormones.

Parent (Tt)

	T	t
T	TT	Tt
t	Tt	tt

Parent (Tt) *(vertical label on left)*

· ·

TT: **25%**

Tt: **50%**

tt: **25%**

· ·

Choice **B** is the only false statement. The endocrine system does not have anything to do with maintaining homeostasis in the body.

What common terms are used for pathogens?

. . . .

What are some of the ways that disease can spread? List three.

. . . .

What statement is NOT true about noninfectious diseases?
A. They are often hereditary and pass as genetic disorders from generation to generation.
B. They are sometimes related to aging.
C. They are often passed on through fungi or bacteria.
D. Environmental factors can cause them.

bacteria, fungi, viruses

. . . .

Answers will vary.

Direct body contact, body fluids, contact with an object that an infected person has touched; through air via coughing, sneezing, dust, spraying of liquid; and via blood are a few of the many ways that disease can be transmitted.

. . . .

Choice **C** is not true. Noninfectious diseases are NOT caused by fungi or bacteria.

What statements are true about the conditions that can cause an epidemic?
- There is plenty of medicine for the disease.
- Diseases develop a resistance to medicine and drugs.
- Environmental conditions are favorable for a specific type of disease.
- Fungi and bacteria are prolific in the area.

. . . .

Place each of the listed items in the appropriate box of the table.

Lower Risk of Disease	Higher Risk of Disease

- smoking
- regular alcohol use
- regular meals of green vegetables
- good portions of protein

- regular sleep
- lack of exercise
- insomnia
- walking
- potato chips for dinner

. . . .

What is the difference between vaccines and antibiotics?

- Diseases develop a resistance to medicine and drugs.
- Environmental conditions are favorable for a specific type of disease.

These two statements are both true about conditions that can cause an epidemic. The first statement is untrue as plenty of medicine would be more likely to prevent an epidemic. The last statement is untrue simply because it is too specific and would only be an environmental condition for a specific type of disease.

· ·

Lower Risk of Disease	Higher Risk of Disease
• regular meals of green vegetables	• smoking
• good portions of protein	• regular alcohol use
• regular sleep	• lack of exercise
• walking	• insomnia
	• potato chips for dinner

· ·

Answers may vary.

Vaccines are made from a dead organism known to cause an immune response (such as a virus) or from a weakened or inactive form of the organism. Antibiotics are chemical compounds designed to kill bacteria without harming cells.

When presented with a weaker or deactivated form of an organism that would normally make a person very ill, the body produces an immune response without causing any illness. Then, if the body ever comes in contact with the strong form of a virus, the _____ that were formed during the immune response to the weaker version are able to fight off disease.

. . . .

What is one of the current dangers of using antibiotics for problems like acne?
A. The acne is not cured.
B. Antibiotics are being used for something inappropriate.
C. Bacteria become resistant to that antibiotic.
D. Bacteria end up on the person's face.

. . . .

What is the best way to describe an ecological network?
A. the physical environment of interacting organisms
B. networking events directed toward exotic, natural environments to support conservation
C. the condition of a region as regards material prosperity
D. the interaction of various species within an ecosystem

When presented with a weaker or deactivated form of an organism that would normally make a person very ill, the body produces an immune response without causing any illness. Then, if the body ever comes in contact with the strong form of a virus, the **antibodies** that were formed during the immune response to the weaker version are able to fight off disease.

· ·

The correct answer is choice **C**, bacteria become resistant to that antibiotic. Someone who took antibiotics for treating acne could accumulate bacteria that are capable of destroying the antibiotic. If that same person became infected with a serious disease that is treated with the same antibiotic, the resistant bacteria could destroy the antibiotic before it was able to act on the disease.

· ·

The correct answer is choice **D**, the interaction of various species within an ecosystem. The other descriptions are for ecosystems, ecotourism, and economics.

Energy flows in an ecosystem through a chain of events called the food chain. Place the following members of the food chain in order of most energy to least energy.
- decomposers
- producers
- secondary consumers
- omnivores
- primary consumers

....

Place the listed organisms into the correct category of the food chain.

Producers	Primary consumers	Secondary consumers	Omnivores	Decomposers

- mouse
- cow
- snake
- ant
- grasshopper
- hawk
- mushroom
- fern
- human
- bacteria
- grass
- cougar

....

1. producers
2. primary consumers
3. secondary consumers
4. omnivores
5. decomposers

. . . .

Producers	Primary consumers	Secondary consumers	Omnivores	Decomposers
grass	grasshopper	snake	human	ant
fern	ant	hawk	mouse	mushroom
	cow	cougar		bacteria
	mouse			

. . . .

A cattle egret forages in a field among a herd of cattle. As the cattle graze and move around the field, insects are disturbed and fly up that are then caught and eaten by the cattle egret. This is an example of _____.

- parasitism
- commensalism
- mutualism

. . . .

Orchids are found in dense tropical forests, where sunlight does not easily reach the floor of the forest. Orchids solve this issue by growing with their base attached to the branches of trees, thus raising themselves up to access adequate sunlight and gather any nutrition that flows down the branches of the tree. As orchids do not grow very large, the tree is not harmed by this attachment. This is an example of _____.

- parasitism
- commensalism
- mutualism

. . . .

Remora fish are small fish that have suckers on their fins allowing them to attach to sharks, whales, and sea turtles. They use the larger sea organism as transportation and protection from other predators. The remora fish also eat any scraps of food that remain when the larger organism eats its prey. This is an example of

_____.

- parasitism
- commensalism
- mutualism

This is an example of **commensalism**.

· ·

This is an example of **commensalism**.

· ·

This is an example of **commensalism**.

The monarch butterfly at the larval stage eats milkweed that is full of a poisonous chemical known as *cardiac glycoside* that is harmful to most vertebrates. Once the butterfly has reached its mature butterfly form, if a bird or other vertebrate eats the butterfly, it finds the butterfly distasteful and will become sick. Because of this, birds and other predators avoid eating monarch butterflies. The relationship between the monarch butterfly and milkweed is an example of _____.
- parasitism
- commensalism
- mutualism

. . . .

Burdocks are weeds that have seeds with long, curved spines attached to them. They are most often found along roadsides, on barren land, and in fields. The spines of the seeds easily catch onto fur and clothing of passing animals and humans, which then carry them and drop them off in other areas. This allows the seeds to disperse while the carriers remain unharmed. This is an example of

_____.
- parasitism
- commensalism
- mutualism

. . . .

A certain kind of bacteria lives within the intestine of humans and other animals. Humans cannot always digest all the foods that they eat. The bacteria eat that food and partially digest it, allowing the human to finish the job. The bacteria get food and the humans benefit by being able to digest the food as well. This an example of

_____.
- parasitism
- commensalism
- mutualism

This is an example of **commensalism**.

. . . .

This is an example of **commensalism**.

. . . .

This is an example of **mutualism**.

Protozoa within the abdomen of a termite help with the digestion of wood. This is an example of _____.
- parasitism
- commensalism
- mutualism

. . . .

A bee lands inside a flower to gather nectar, which is made into food for the hive. The flower happens to have pollen inside of it as well, which ends up covering the hairy body and legs of the bee. When the bee lands on the next flower, some of the pollen that was on its body rubs of into the new flower. This is an example of

_____.
- parasitism
- commensalism
- mutualism

. . . .

Spider crabs live in the shallows of the ocean floor and have greenish-brown algae living on their backs. This allows the crabs to blend into their environment, avoiding notice by predators, while the algae have a solid place to live. This an example of _____.
- parasitism
- commensalism
- mutualism

This is an example of **mutualism**.

. . . .

This is an example of **mutualism**.

. . . .

This is an example of **mutualism**.

What is the term for the maximum population size that an environment can sustain?

. . . .

Read the description of a symbiotic relationship and select the correct term for the relationship from the following list.

Mistletoe attaches to spruce trees. Using specialized structures, mistletoe penetrates into and extracts water and nutrients from the tree's branches.
- commensalism
- mutualism
- parasitism

. . . .

Read the description of a symbiotic relationship and select the correct term for the relationship from the following list.

E. coli bacteria live within the intestinal tract of humans, obtaining nutrients from the food particles that pass through the intestines. Vitamin K produced by the *E. coli* is absorbed through the intestinal walls for use in the human body.
- commensalism
- mutualism
- parasitism

This is called **carrying capacity**.

. . . .

The symbiotic relationship exhibited by mistletoe and spruce trees is **parasitism**. The mistletoe receives a benefit in the form of a source of nutrients and water. The spruce tree is harmed because it loses nutrients and water, which can eventually lead to the death of the tree. Parasitism is occurring when one organism benefits (mistletoe) and the other organism is harmed (spruce tree).

. . . .

The symbiotic relationship exhibited by E. coli and humans is **mutualism**. The E. coli receive a benefit in the form of nutrients and a habitat in which to live. The human also receives a benefit because the E. coli produce vitamin K, which is then used within the human body. Mutualism is occurring when both organisms benefit.

Refer to the following passage to answer the next two questions.

Veterinary clinics often treat pets with illnesses resulting from parasitism. Three common parasites diagnosed in dogs are the dog flea, deer tick, and *Cheyletiella* mites.

Dog fleas and deer ticks both feed on the host animal's (dog's) blood, and can transmit diseases to the host animal through their bites. Dog fleas lay their eggs on the host animal's body, and can survive on the host animal or on surfaces the animal comes in contact with, such as bedding. Deer ticks lay their eggs on the ground and attach to the host animal only while feeding.

Cheyletiella mites live within and feed on the keratin layer of the host animal's skin. *Cheyletiella* mites reproduce on the host animal, and can survive away from the host animal for only short periods of time.

According to the passage, all the dog parasites gain which benefit from their symbiotic relationships with the host dogs?
A. a habitat for living
B. a vector for disease
C. a source of nutrients
D. a site for reproduction

A veterinary technician is preparing to examine a dog suspected of having *Cheyletiella* mites. Which precaution would most effectively prevent the transmission of mites to other animals in the clinic?
A. administering a vaccine to the infected dog
B. wearing disposable gloves while examining the dog
C. avoiding contact with open wounds on the dog
D. sterilizing the exam room prior to examining the dog

The correct answer is **C, a source of nutrients**. The fleas and ticks obtain nutrients from the host animal's blood, and the mites obtain nutrients from the host animal's skin. Although the fleas and mites may live and reproduce on the host animal's body, the ticks do not. And while parasites can transmit diseases to the host animal, this does not provide a benefit to the parasite.

• •

The correct answer is choice **B**. The passage states that *Cheyletiella* mites live within the outermost layer of the dog's skin, and have difficulty surviving away from the host animal's body. Wearing gloves that are disposed of after examining the dog helps prevent mites transferred to the technician's hands from being transmitted to other animals in the clinic.

Vaccines can be administered to non-infected individuals to prevent the transmission of diseases caused by viruses, but mites are arthropods that live on the host animal's body, and cannot be eliminated with a vaccine. Avoiding contact with open wounds would help prevent the transmission of bloodborne pathogens, such as those transmitted by fleas and ticks, but would not help with the transmission of mites. Also, sterilizing the exam room after, not before, examining the infected dog could help prevent the transmission of mites to other animals in the clinic.

• •

The table compares characteristics for four different groups of plants. A "1" indicates the characteristic is present and a "0" indicates the characteristic is absent.

Plant Type	Vascular Tissue	Seeds	Flowers
Conifers	1	1	0
Ferns	1	0	0
Flowering Plants	1	1	1
Mosses	0	0	0

A *cladogram* illustrates the relatedness of organisms based on shared characteristics. Branches below a given characteristic represent organisms that do not exhibit that characteristic. Branches above a given characteristic represent organisms that do exhibit that characteristic. Each branch represents one plant type.

Use the information in the table to organize the plant types onto the appropriate branches in the cladogram.
- **conifers**
- **ferns**
- **flowering plants**
- **mosses**

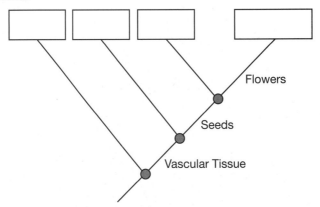

In a cladogram, the group that exhibits the fewest characteristics is listed on the bottom left branch, and the group exhibiting the most characteristics is listed on the top right branch.

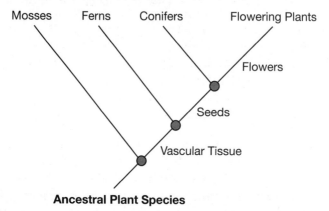

Ancestral Plant Species

Mosses are placed on the first (lowest) branch because they exhibit none of the characteristics listed in the table. Ferns contain vascular tissue, so are listed on the second branch. Confers are on the third branch because they contain vascular tissue and produce seeds. Flowering plants exhibit all three characteristics listed in the table, so are on the fourth (highest) branch.

The food web for a woodland ecosystem bordering an area of farmland is shown here.

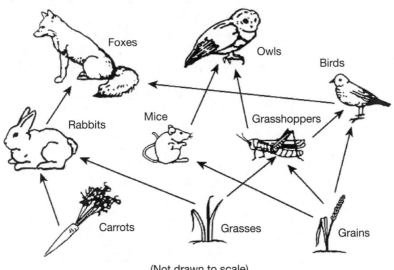

(Not drawn to scale)

According to the concept of consumers and producers, rabbits are considered primary consumers because they
A. feed on grasses and carrots
B. are consumed by foxes only
C. compete with grasshoppers only
D. are the only consumer of carrots

The correct answer is choice **A**. A primary level consumer feeds on producers. Producers, such as plants, make their own food using energy from sunlight. Rabbits feed on two producers, carrots and grasses, making rabbits a primary level consumer.

An organism's feeding level is determined by how it obtains its food, not by the organisms that it provides food for. Although the rabbits in the food web are consumed by foxes, this does not determine the rabbits' feeding level. Competition with other organisms does not affect how an organism's feeding level is classified. Also, the presence of other organisms that consume the same food source does not affect how an organism's feeding level is classified.

The food web for a woodland ecosystem bordering an area of farmland is shown here.

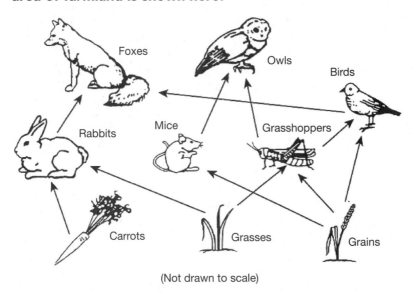

(Not drawn to scale)

Which three organisms in the food web obtain energy directly or indirectly from grasshoppers?
A. owls, birds, and mice
B. owls, birds, and grains
C. foxes, rabbits, and mice
D. foxes, owls, and birds

. . . .

A bacterial disease has destroyed most of the farm's carrot crop for the past two seasons. As a result, the rabbit population has been forced to rely more heavily on grasses for a food source.

Explain how this disruption is likely to affect the rest of the ecosystem's food web. Include multiple pieces of evidence and discuss specific populations (other than carrots and rabbits) as examples to support your answer.

. . . .

The correct answer is choice **D**. An organism provides energy to all organisms above it in the food web. In this food web, the grasshoppers provide energy to the birds, owls, and foxes. The birds and owls obtain energy directly when they consume the grasshoppers. The foxes obtain energy indirectly when they consume birds that previously consumed grasshoppers.

Although owls and birds obtain energy from grasshoppers, mice do not obtain energy from grasshoppers. Grains provide energy to grasshoppers; they do not obtain energy from grasshoppers. Rabbits and mice do not obtain energy from grasshoppers either directly or indirectly.

GED® TEST SCIENCE FLASH REVIEW

Answers may vary.

The interrelatedness of populations in the food web makes it likely that all populations will be affected in some way by the shift in the rabbits' feeding habits. The rabbits' increased reliance on grasses will cause a domino effect on the availability of food for all primary consumers. Since grasshoppers directly compete with rabbits for grasses, the availability of grasses for grasshoppers may be limited. As a result, grasshoppers would likely increase their dependence on grains, decreasing the availability of this food source for birds and mice. The overall increase in competition among primary consumers may cause some decreases in population sizes, which would also limit the population sizes of higher-level consumers.

The table illustrates the range of normal body temperatures in Fahrenheit for different age groups.

Normal Body Temperature	
Age Group	Temperature (in ° Fahrenheit)
Newborn	97.7°–99.5°
Infants (1 year or less)	97.0°–99.0°
Children (1–17 years)	97.5°–98.6°
Adults (above 18 years)	97.6°–99°
Elders (above 70 years)	96.8°–97.5°

The formula for converting Fahrenheit to Celsius is shown here.

$$(°F - 32) \times \frac{5}{9} = °C$$

The normal body temperature range of a newborn baby is _____°C to _____°C. (You may use a calculator to complete this question.)

. . . .

The normal body temperature range of a newborn baby is **36.5°C** to **37.5°C**.

Blank 1: The formula for converting temperature from Fahrenheit to Celsius is given as $(°F - 32) \times \frac{5}{9} = °C$. Replacing the lower variable °F with 97.7 and solving gives $(97.7 - 32) \times \frac{5}{9} = 36.5$.

Blank 2: The formula for converting temperature from Fahrenheit to Celsius is given as $(°F - 32) \times \frac{5}{9} = °C$. Replacing the lower variable °F with 99.5 and solving gives $(99.5 - 32) \times \frac{5}{9} = 37.5$.

The process of meiosis is depicted in the following diagram.

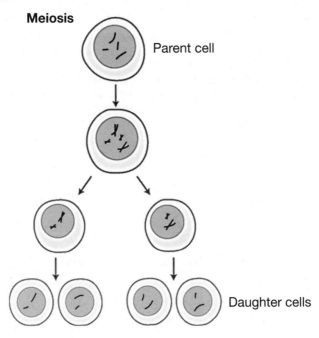

Meiosis

Parent cell

Daughter cells

The daughter cells produced during meiosis are used for what purpose?

A. growth
B. tissue repair
C. differentiation
D. reproduction

As indicated in the diagram, the daughter cells produced during meiosis each have half the total number of chromosomes as the parent cell has. These daughter cells, called gametes, are used for choice **D, reproduction**. When reproduction occurs, two gametes (egg and sperm) unite to create a cell with a full set of chromosomes.

To allow an organism to grow larger and repair tissues, the daughter cells produced must be identical to the parent cell. Cells used for growth and tissue repair are produced by the process of mitosis. Cell differentiation occurs when a single, non-specialized cell is converted to a specialized cell type, like a blood cell or skin cell. No daughter cells are produced during the differentiation process.

Meiosis produces cells containing one chromosome from each chromosome pair. This diagram shows the chromosome combinations that can be produced from a cell containing two pairs of chromosomes.

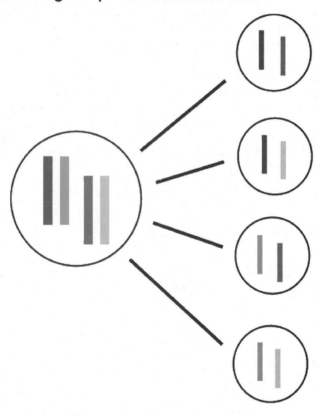

A barley plant has seven pairs of chromosomes. How many unique combinations of chromosomes can result from meiosis in barley?

A. 7
B. 14
C. 49
D. 128

The correct answer is choice **D, 128**. Each new cell created by meiosis must contain one chromosome from each of the seven chromosome pairs. As illustrated in the diagram, these single chromosomes can be combined in multiple ways. To determine the total number of unique chromosome combinations, the number of chromosomes in each set (pair) must be multiplied. Seven sets of two chromosomes each means that 7 twos must be multiplied ($2 \times 2 \times 2 \times 2 \times 2 \times 2 \times 2 = 128$) to determine the total number of unique chromosome combinations possible.

There are seven total chromosomes in a cell produced by meiosis, but the specific chromosome present from each chromosome pair can vary. Two chromosomes in each of seven pairs provides a total of 14 chromosomes, but since the specific chromosome present from each pair can vary, multiplying 7×7 does not provide the total number of chromosome combinations possible. To determine this, the number of chromosomes in each pair must be multiplied by the number of chromosomes in each other pair.

A student draws the model shown here to represent the process of aerobic respiration.

Which change would improve the accuracy of the student's model?
A. connecting all the circles to each other to show bonds
B. moving the energy symbol to the left side of the equation
C. adding five triangles to balance the right side of the equation
D. making the rectangles smaller to show relative molecular sizes

. . . .

The energy produced by respiration is in what form?
A. ATP
B. oxygen
C. glucose
D. carbon dioxide

. . . .

The correct answer is choice **C**. The products of respiration are six molecules of carbon dioxide, six molecules of water, and energy. On the right side of the model, six rectangles are present, but only one triangle. To accurately represent a balanced equation, all molecules must be represented in the model.

The circles represent the six molecules of the reactant oxygen. Connecting the circles would not improve the model's accuracy because separate molecules are not bound to each other. Energy is a product of the respiration reaction, and is therefore appropriately placed on the right side of the equation. Moving the energy symbol to the left side of the equation would indicate that energy is a reactant. Reducing the size of the rectangles is not the most needed change, since the other molecules are not represented to scale.

. . . .

The correct answer is choice **A**. The purpose of respiration is to convert energy into a form that is usable by cells. Respiration produces ATP, a high-energy molecule, which the cell can use to carry out cellular functions.

Oxygen is a reactant, not a product, of aerobic respiration, and does not provide energy for the cell. Respiration uses the glucose in food to produce ATP. Respiration does not produce glucose. And, though respiration does produce carbon dioxide, this molecule does not provide energy for the cell.

. . . .

GED® TEST SCIENCE FLASH REVIEW

Explain the benefit of having two pathways for respiration in the human body.

· ·

Answers may vary.

The human body may utilize two different pathways to carry out respiration. The presence of two different pathways is valuable because it allows a cell to choose the pathway that best meets its current energy needs. Aerobic respiration produces the greatest amount of ATP per glucose molecule. Under normal conditions with adequate oxygen, this pathway provides the greatest possible amount of energy to the cell. Anaerobic respiration produces much less ATP per glucose molecule, but does not require oxygen. Under strenuous conditions when the cell demands energy faster than the oxygen supply can be replenished, this pathway provides enough energy to maintain cell functions. The ability to switch between aerobic and anaerobic pathways allows the human body to function properly under varying conditions.

· ·

Artificial selection is the process of breeding plants or animals to increase the occurrence of desired traits. Farmers use artificial selection to produce new crop species from existing plant species. The diagram illustrates six crop species that have been derived from the common wild mustard plant.

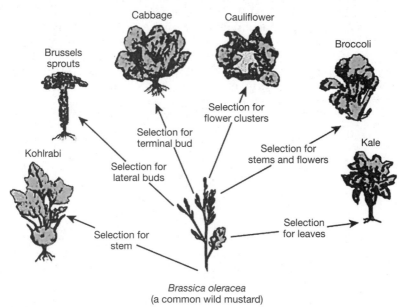

Brussels sprouts

Cabbage

Cauliflower

Broccoli

Selection for flower clusters

Selection for terminal bud

Selection for stems and flowers

Kale

Kohlrabi

Selection for lateral buds

Selection for leaves

Selection for stem

Brassica oleracea
(a common wild mustard)

Based on the information in the passage, how did farmers produce kale?

A. Farmers removed the stems and flowers from mustard plants as they grew.

B. Farmers allowed only wild mustard plants with large leaves to reproduce.

C. Farmers bred small-leafed plants with large-leafed plants to increase leaf size.

D. Farmers prevented wild mustard plants with large leaves from reproducing.

The correct answer is choice **B**. Kale is a leafy crop species. According to the diagram, wild mustard plants were selected for leaves to produce kale. This means that wild mustard plants that had large leaves were specifically bred together to increase leaf size. This selective breeding over multiple generations led to a new species (kale) characterized by large leaves.

Plants with desired characteristics (large leaves for kale) must be bred together to produce offspring plants with those characteristics. Removing stems and flowers from existing mustard plants will not increase leaf size in subsequent generations. Breeding small-leafed plants and large-leafed plants allows the possibility that offspring will have either small or large leaves. To ensure offspring have the best chances of large leaves, large-leafed plants should be bred together. Preventing plants with large leaves from growing works to remove the large-leaf trait from subsequent generations rather than increase its appearance.

Every person has two copies, or alleles, of the ABO blood type gene. A person's ABO blood type is determined by their specific combination of alleles. The table shows the allele combinations that cause the four different ABO blood types.

Blood Type	Genotype
A	I^AI^A or I^Ai
B	I^BI^B or I^Bi
AB	I^AI^B
O	ii

A mother's allele combination is I^Ai and a father's allele combination is I^AI^B. Which of the following statements is true about the blood type of their first child?

A. The child will have the same blood type as the mother.
B. The child cannot have the father's blood type.
C. The child will have a blood type different from both parents.
D. The child cannot have blood type O.

. . . .

Choice **D** is the only true statement. The blood type O can only be produced by the allele combination ii. A child receives one allele from each parent. Since the mother has an i but the father does not, the allele combination ii is not possible for their children.

Based on the table, the mother's blood type is A. The child can receive I^A or i from the mother and I^A from the father, resulting in type A blood caused by the possible allele combinations I^AI^A or I^Ai. However, the child could receive I^B from the father, which would result in a blood type different from the mother. Based on the table, the father has blood type AB. The child can receive I^A from the mother and I^B from the father, resulting in the possible allele combination I^AI^B. This allele combination will produce the same blood type as the father's. Also, based on the table, the mother's blood type is A and the father's is AB. The child can receive I^A or i from the mother and I^A from the father, resulting in type A blood caused by the possible allele combinations I^AI^A or I^Ai. The child can receive I^A from the mother and I^B from the father, resulting in the blood type AB caused by the possible allele combination I^AI^B. This means it is possible for the child to have the same blood type as either one of the parents.

Blood glucose levels are tightly regulated in the human body by the hormones insulin and glucagon. When glucose levels become too high or low, the pancreas produces the appropriate hormone to return the body to homeostasis. The diagram shows the feedback mechanism for regulating blood glucose levels.

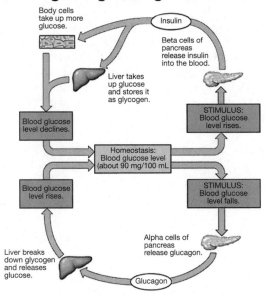

Diabetes mellitus is a disease in which the pancreas is unable to produce the insulin needed to regulate blood glucose levels. What result would occur from providing an insulin injection to a diabetic person with high blood sugar?

A. The insulin travels to the liver where it binds to and destroys excess glucose in the bloodstream.

B. The insulin signals the pancreas to produce glucagon, which increases the level of glucose in the bloodstream.

C. The insulin causes the liver to convert glucose to glycogen, removing excess glucose from the bloodstream.

D. The insulin breaks down glycogen into glucose, releasing stored glucose into the bloodstream.

The correct answer is choice **C**. According to the diagram, when a person's blood glucose level rises, the pancreas secretes insulin. The insulin signals body cells to absorb glucose from the blood, and signals the liver to convert excess glucose into the storage molecule glycogen. These processes remove excess glucose from the blood, returning the blood glucose level to homeostasis. Insulin injected into a diabetic person initiates the same pathway as insulin produced in the pancreas of a healthy person.

Insulin signals the liver to convert and store excess glucose as glycogen, not to destroy the glucose. Insulin and glucagon do not signal each other, but perform opposite functions. Insulin functions to decrease blood glucose levels, while glucagon functions to increase levels. Glucagon signals the breakdown of glycogen into glucose when blood glucose levels are low. Insulin signals the conversion of glucose to glycogen when blood glucose levels are high.

How would you describe ATP?

. . . .

What are capillaries?

. . . .

What is a cytoskeleton?

Adenosine triphosphate (ATP) is a chemical that is considered to be the "fuel" or energy source for an organism.

. . . .

Vascular tissues that receive blood from the arterioles and release the blood to the venuoles.

. . . .

Organelles that are the internal "bones" of the cell. Cytoskeletons exist in thick and thin tubules.

What does DNA stand for?

. . . .

What is gel electrophoresis?

. . . .

DNA is the abbreviation for **deoxyribonucleic acid**. It contains all genetic material for an organism. The smallest units of DNA are called nucleotides.

· ·

A process used in laboratories to determine the genetic makeup of DNA strands. This process involves the movement of chromosomes through a gel from one pole to the other. Magnetism is used to pull the chromosomes through the gel.

· ·

Refer to the following passage to answer the next nine questions.

Anatomy of Muscles

Muscles are made of bundles of cells wrapped in connective tissue called *fascicles*. Each bundle contains many cylindrical muscle cells or muscle fibers. Like other cells, muscle fibers have mitochondria that provide energy, a plasma membrane that separates the inside and outside of the cell, and endoplasmic reticulum, where proteins are made. However, muscle cells are different from other cells in several ways. First, muscle cells have more than one nucleus. Second, the muscle cell's plasma membrane surrounds bundles of cylindrical myofibrils that contain protein filaments and regularly folds into the deep parts of the fiber to form a transverse tubule or T-tubule. Third, the muscle cell's endoplasmic reticulum is called sarcoplasmic reticulum; it is regularly structured, envelops the myofibrils, and ends near the T-tubule in sacs called terminal cisternae.

Look at the title of the passage. The title often previews what the reading will be about. What does this title reveal about the passage?

. . . .

Look at each sentence in the passage. Look at the subject of each sentence (we are showing the parts of each one, not the whole):
1. **Muscles are made of bundles of cells. . . .**
2. **Each bundle contains many cylindrical muscle cells. . . .**
3. **Muscle fibers have mitochondria . . . , plasma membrane . . . , and endoplasmic reticulum. . . .**
4. **Muscle cells are different from other cells in several ways.**
5. **Muscle cells have more than one nucleus.**
6. **The muscle cell's plasma membrane surrounds bundles of. . . .**
7. **The muscle cell's endoplasmic reticulum is called sarcoplasmic reticulum. . . .**

What do the subjects of the sentences have in common?

. . . .

The title tells us that the passage is going to be about the structure or anatomy of muscles.

· ·

They all have **muscle** in common.

· ·

The pattern of *muscle* as the subject of each sentence also provides a clue as to the subject of the entire passage. What do you think is the main purpose of this passage?

. . . .

What is the shape of a muscle cell?
A. sphere
B. cylinder
C. disc
D. cube

. . . .

Which is a difference between a muscle cell and another type of cell?
A. Only muscle cells have mitochondria.
B. The plasma membrane separates the inside from the outside of the muscle cell.
C. Muscle cells have more than one nucleus.
D. Muscle cells do not have endoplasmic reticulum.

The main purpose of this passage is to **describe the structure of muscles**. Both the title and the subjects of each sentence indicate this information.

· ·

The correct answer is choice **B**, **cylinder**. The second sentence mentions that bundles contain many *cylindrical* muscle cells.

· ·

The correct answer is choice **C**. The fifth sentence of the passage states that "First, muscle cells have more than one nucleus."

"Muscles are made of bundles of cells wrapped in connective tissue called *fascicles*." What word helps you with context for the word *fascicles*?

. . . .

"Each bundle contains many cylindrical muscle cells or muscle fibers." What word helps you with context for the phrase *muscle fibers*?

. . . .

"Like other cells, muscle fibers have mitochondria that provide energy, a plasma membrane that separates the inside and outside of the cell, and endoplasmic reticulum, where proteins are made." What helps you with context for the phrase *endoplasmic reticulum*?

The word *called* connects the term with its definition.

· ·

The word *or* connects the term *fiber* with another more familiar term, *cell*.

· ·

The comma connects the term *endoplasmic reticulum* with an explanation of its purpose, *where proteins are made.*

"Like other cells, muscle fibers have mitochondria that provide energy, a plasma membrane that separates the inside and outside of the cell, and endoplasmic reticulum, where proteins are made." How do you get context for the phrase *plasma membrane*?

. . . .

The word *that* separates a clause that can convey important information. For example, "a plasma membrane that separates the inside and outside of the cell" reveals that the function of the plasma membrane is to separate the inside from the outside of the cell.

Refer to the following passage to answer the next three questions.

In sexual reproduction, DNA is contributed by two parents with the goal of producing genetically distinct offspring. In most organisms, sexual reproduction includes a special form of cell division called meiosis, which results in the reduction of the number of chromosomes. Cells with only one complete set, or pair, of chromosomes are called haploid. Haploid cells are the reproductive cells, called either gametes or sex cells. Cells that contain two complete sets of chromosomes are called diploid. Almost all the cells in your body are diploid. Humans have 46 chromosomes or 23 pairs in each body cell. In sexual reproduction, two haploid cells, sperm and egg, combine to form a diploid cell, a zygote, which then develops into the offspring organism.

Haploid and diploid are designated by the algebraic notations n and $2n$. Either number can be calculated when the other number is known. The table shows some of the haploid or diploid numbers for various organisms.

Organism	Haploid Number (n)	Diploid Number ($2n$)
Chimpanzee	24	
Earthworm	18	
Honeybee		56
Human		46
Onion		16

How many chromosomes are in the gametes of an onion?

. . . .

What is the difference between the number of chromosomes in non-sex cells of a human and a chimpanzee?
A. 1
B. 2
C. 22
D. 80

. . . .

There are **8** chromosomes in the gametes of an onion. A gamete is a haploid cell and has half the number of chromosomes as the diploid cell. A diploid cell of an onion has 16 chromosomes, so an onion's gamete must have $\frac{16}{2}$ or 8 chromosomes.

· ·

The correct answer is choice **B, 2**. A non-sex cell is a diploid cell. The diploid cell of a chimpanzee has 48 chromosomes ($24 \times 2 = 48$). The diploid cell of a human has 46 chromosomes (the number is in the table). So, the difference in chromosomes between a human and a chimpanzee is 2 chromosomes ($48 - 46 = 2$).

· ·

Which process produces a sperm or an egg?
A. trichinosis
B. meiosis
C. mitosis
D. metamorphosis

. . . .

Jim has two overweight dachshunds. He sees an advertisement for a new reduced-calorie dog food that claims to allow the dogs to eat normally, but still lose weight.

Propose a hypothesis to test the claim in the advertisement. What is the hypothesis?

Hypothesis: If _____, then _____.

. . . .

Jim has two overweight dachshunds. He sees an advertisement for a new reduced-calorie dog food that claims to allow the dogs to eat normally, but still lose weight.

Propose an experiment to test the claim in the advertisement. What is the suggested experiment?

The correct answer is choice **B**, **meiosis**. Sperm and egg cells are gametes, which are haploid cells that have half the number of chromosomes. The second sentence of the passage states that "In most organisms, sexual reproduction includes a special form of cell division called meiosis, which results in the reduction of the number of chromosomes."

. . . .

The wording of your hypothesis may vary.

If **Jim feeds one dog the new dog food**, then **that dog should lose weight compared to the other**.

. . . .

The wording of your experiment may vary.

Feed both dogs at the same time with the same amount of dog food. Substitute the new reduced-calorie dog food for the normal dog food for one of the dogs. Separate the dogs when they are eating so that one dog does not eat the other's food. Measure the weight of both dogs weekly over the course of six weeks.

Jim has two overweight dachshunds. He sees an advertisement for a new reduced-calorie dog food that claims to allow the dogs to eat normally, but still lose weight.

Propose a predicted result of an experiment to test the claim in the advertisement. What is the predicted result?

. . . .

The wording of your predicted result may vary.

The dog eating reduced-calorie dog food should lose weight compared to the dog eating normal dog food.

. . . .

A coffee retailer wants to know whether customers prefer brand A or brand B coffee. So, he sets up a blind taste test. He prepares pots of coffee with equal volumes using the same amount of coffee, either brand A or brand B. The coffees are brewed at the same temperature and the same time. The retailer knows which pot contains brand A and which contains brand B. He gives the pots to a clerk. A clerk pours two sample cups of equal volume for each customer, one from each pot. The pots of coffee are not labeled and the clerk does not know which coffee she is serving. For 100 customers, she has each customer taste each sample cup of coffee and write which choice he or she preferred. The clerk tallies the choices and gives the tally to the coffee retailer.

Identify the controlled and uncontrolled factors in the experiment.

Assign the correct variables into each box:

Independent Variable
Dependent Variable
Controls

- amount of coffee in each pot
- coffee brand served
- coffee temperature
- coffee brewing time
- volume of coffee pots
- customer's preferred coffee brand
- amount of coffee served
- The clerk does not know what brand she is serving.

Independent Variable
coffee brand served
Dependent Variable
customer's preferred coffee brand
Controls
volume of coffee pots
coffee temperature
coffee brewing time
amount of coffee in each pot
amount of coffee served
The clerk does not know what brand she is serving.

Experiment: Does fertilizer A help plants grow faster than fertilizer B?

Process: First, identify what variables will be tested and what variables should be controlled. Fertilizers A and B should be applied to the same type of plant. This makes the type of plant one of your controls.

Should all the plants be fertilized?

. . . .

Experiment: Does fertilizer A help plants grow faster than fertilizer B?

Process: First, identify what variables will be tested and what variables should be controlled. Fertilizers A and B should be applied to the same type of plant. This makes the type of plant one of your controls.

Should one plant get more sunlight or water or be exposed to different temperatures for different times than the other experimental plant?

. . . .

Experiment: Does fertilizer A help plants grow faster than fertilizer B?

Process: First, identify what variables will be tested and what variables should be controlled. Fertilizers A and B should be applied to the same type of plant. This makes the type of plant one of your controls.

The amount of fertilizer being applied _____.
- **should be the same**
- **can be different**

No. There should be a control that has no fertilizer for comparison to make sure that both types of fertilizer are working.

· ·

No. Water, temperature, and amount of light should also be controls, as well as the length of the experiment (time).

· ·

The amount of fertilizer being applied **should be the same**. It should also be controlled in the experiment.

Experiment: Does fertilizer A help plants grow faster than fertilizer B?

Process: First, identify what variables will be tested and what variables should be controlled. Fertilizers A and B should be applied to the same type of plant. This makes the type of plant one of your controls.

The independent variable will be _____.

. . . .

Experiment: Does fertilizer A help plants grow faster than fertilizer B?

Process: First, identify what variables will be tested and what variables should be controlled. Fertilizers A and B should be applied to the same type of plant. This makes the type of plant one of your controls.

The dependent variable will be _____.

. . . .

Experiment: Does fertilizer A help plants grow faster than fertilizer B?

Process: First, identify what variables will be tested and what variables should be controlled. Fertilizers A and B should be applied to the same type of plant. This makes the type of plant one of your controls.

How will you measure the plant growth (height, mass, etc.)? What instrument will you use?

The independent variable will be **the type of fertilizer**. The type of fertilizer will act as the independent variable because you want to know what effect it has on the plant.

. . . .

The dependent variable will be **the plant growth**. The plant growth will act as the dependent variable, the factor observed and measured to see if it is affected by the fertilizer.

. . . .

Responses may vary.

Measuring the plant height is the easiest way to measure growth. You can measure the height with a metric ruler.

Experiment: Does fertilizer A help plants grow faster than fertilizer B?

Process: First, identify what variables will be tested and what variables should be controlled. Fertilizers A and B should be applied to the same type of plant. This makes the type of plant one of your controls.

How many plants would make the best representative population sample for this experiment?

A. 2
B. 10
C. 100
D. 1,000

· ·

The correct answer is choice **B**, **10**. Of the choices, this makes the most sense; there are a significant number of plants in each group to be able to observe shared differences.

Refer to the following passage to answer the next 12 questions.

Today, about 30% of the children in the United States are overweight or obese. This puts them at increased risk for diseases such as diabetes (measured by fasting glucose levels) and heart disease (due to high cholesterol levels). The local county health department wants to improve the health of the young children in the community. Most research indicates that changing diet and exercise is the best way to reduce obesity in children, but they suspect that children may not be willing to change both diet and exercise.

First, identify what variables will be tested and what variables should be controlled. Should all the children be placed in a program of diet and exercise?

. . . .

First, identify what variables will be tested and what variables should be controlled. Should both diet and exercise be only tested together?

. . . .

The county health department undertakes a new program to encourage children to eat better and exercise. They enroll 200 children in a six-month program and plan to set up three groups:
- **Group 1: Diet and exercise**
- **Group 2: Diet only**
- **Group 3: Exercise only**

The county health department hypothesizes that the children in the diet and exercise group will have the best outcomes.

Should one child participate in dieting and exercising longer than the other experimental children?

No. There should be a control that has no diet or exercise for comparison to make sure that both diet and exercise are working.

· ·

No. Each variable of diet and exercise must also be tested separately.

· ·

No. The length of the experiment (time) should be a control in the experiment.

The county health department undertakes a new program to encourage children to eat better and exercise. They enroll 200 children in a six-month program and plan to set up three groups:
- Group 1: Diet and exercise
- Group 2: Diet only
- Group 3: Exercise only

The county health department hypothesizes that the children in the diet and exercise group will have the best outcomes.

The amount of diet and exercise being applied _____.
- should be the same
- can be different

. . . .

The county health department undertakes a new program to encourage children to eat better and exercise. They enroll 200 children in a six-month program and plan to set up three groups:
- Group 1: Diet and exercise
- Group 2: Diet only
- Group 3: Exercise only

The county health department hypothesizes that the children in the diet and exercise group will have the best outcomes.

The independent variables will be _____.

. . . .

The amount of diet and exercise being applied **should be the same**. It should also be controlled in the experiment.

· ·

The independent variables will be **application of diet and exercise, just diet**, or **just exercise**.

The application of diet and exercise, just diet, or just exercise will act as the independent variables because you want to know what effect each has on the children.

· ·

The county health department undertakes a new program to encourage children to eat better and exercise. They enroll 200 children in a six-month program and plan to set up three groups:
- Group 1: Diet and exercise
- Group 2: Diet only
- Group 3: Exercise only

The county health department hypothesizes that the children in the diet and exercise group will have the best outcomes.

The dependent variables will be _____.

. . . .

The county health department undertakes a new program to encourage children to eat better and exercise. They enroll 200 children in a six-month program and plan to set up three groups:
- Group 1: Diet and exercise
- Group 2: Diet only
- Group 3: Exercise only

The county health department hypothesizes that the children in the diet and exercise group will have the best outcomes.

How would the 200 children enrolled in the six-month program be best divided up?

. . . .

The dependent variables will be **weight, cholesterol levels,** and **fasting blood glucose levels** of each group. The weight, cholesterol levels, and fasting blood glucose levels of each group will act as the dependent variables, the factors observed and measured to see whether they are affected by the application of diet and exercise.

· ·

The county health department should randomly assign the 200 children to one of three experimental groups, as well as a control group, as follows:

- Group 1: Diet and exercise (50 children)

- Group 2: Diet only (50 children)

- Group 3: Exercise only (50 children)

- Control group: No change in daily routine (50 children)

· ·

The county health department undertakes a new program to encourage children to eat better and exercise. They enroll 200 children in a six-month program and plan to set up three groups:
- Group 1: Diet and exercise
- Group 2: Diet only
- Group 3: Exercise only

The county health department hypothesizes that the children in the diet and exercise group will have the best outcomes.

What measurements would need to be taken before the experiment begins?

. . . .

The county health department undertakes a new program to encourage children to eat better and exercise. They enroll 200 children in a six-month program and plan to set up three groups:
- Group 1: Diet and exercise
- Group 2: Diet only
- Group 3: Exercise only

The county health department hypothesizes that the children in the diet and exercise group will have the best outcomes.

What would be a reasonable description of the experiment and checks for Group 1?

. . . .

The health department would have to take measurements of all the children before the intervention begins, at two months, and at six months to measure the change over time. They would take height, weight, cholesterol levels, and fasting blood glucose levels. They would also need to ask questions about the diet of the children and the amount of exercise they do on a daily basis.

. . . .

The children in Group 1 (diet and exercise) would be on a diet lower in fat and sugar (weekly menus provided by the health department) and would be asked to double the amount of exercise they do in a week (e.g., if they normally exercise 20 minutes per week they would be asked to exercise 40 minutes per week). Parents would be asked to keep a food log and record the exercise on a daily basis.

. . . .

The county health department undertakes a new program to encourage children to eat better and exercise. They enroll 200 children in a six-month program and plan to set up three groups:
• Group 1: Diet and exercise
• Group 2: Diet only
• Group 3: Exercise only

The county health department hypothesizes that the children in the diet and exercise group will have the best outcomes.

What would be a reasonable description of the experiment and checks for Group 2?

. . . .

The county health department undertakes a new program to encourage children to eat better and exercise. They enroll 200 children in a six-month program and plan to set up three groups:
• Group 1: Diet and exercise
• Group 2: Diet only
• Group 3: Exercise only

The county health department hypothesizes that the children in the diet and exercise group will have the best outcomes.

What would be a reasonable description of the experiment and checks for Group 3?

. . . .

The children in Group 2 (diet change only) would be on the same reduced fat and lower sugar diet as the children in group 1, but would not change their exercise routine. Parents would be asked to keep a food log and record the exercise on a daily basis.

· ·

The children in Group 3 (exercise change only) would not be asked to change their diets, but would be asked to double the amount of exercise they do on a weekly basis, as in Group 1. Parents would be asked to keep a food log and record the exercise on a daily basis.

· ·

The county health department undertakes a new program to encourage children to eat better and exercise. They enroll 200 children in a six-month program and plan to set up three groups:

- Group 1: Diet and exercise
- Group 2: Diet only
- Group 3: Exercise only

The county health department hypothesizes that the children in the diet and exercise group will have the best outcomes.

What would be a reasonable description of the experiment and checks for the control group?

. . . .

The children in the control group would not be asked to change anything, but parents would be asked to keep a food log and record the exercise on a daily basis.

. . . .

Wolves crossed an ice bridge from Canada to the Isle Royale, Michigan, and established a population. Moose were native to the island. Since the 1950s, ecologists have studied the moose and wolf populations on the island. The population data are shown in the graph.

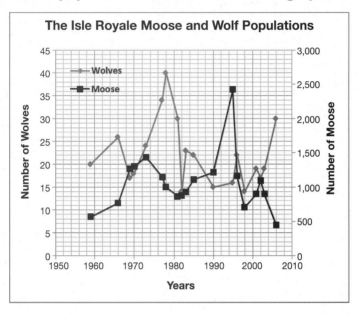

The Isle Royale Moose and Wolf Populations

Ecologists noted several events, which are summarized in the table.

Year	Event
1964–1972	Mild winters
1972–1980	Severe winters
1981–1984	Humans inadvertently introduce canine parvovirus to the island
1997	Severe winter, outbreak of moose ticks, new wolf emigrates from Canada

Based on the information, what can you conclude about the relationship between moose (prey) and wolves (predator) between 1959 and 1995?

. . . .

Your wording may vary.

The increase in the moose population (1964–1972) induced increased predation by wolves and a subsequent increase in the wolf population. Once the wolf population crashed from disease (1981–1984), the moose population recovered and increased through 1995.

Wolves crossed an ice bridge from Canada to the Isle Royale, Michigan, and established a population. Moose were native to the island. Since the 1950s, ecologists have studied the moose and wolf populations on the island. The population data are shown in the graph.

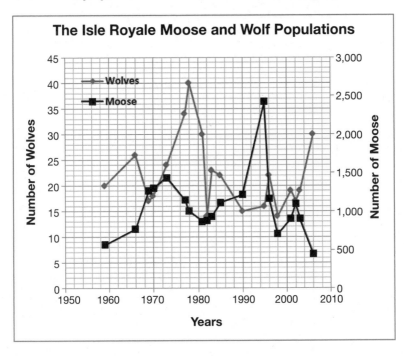

The Isle Royale Moose and Wolf Populations

Ecologists noted several events, which are summarized in the table.

Year	Event
1964–1972	Mild winters
1972–1980	Severe winters
1981–1984	Humans inadvertently introduce canine parvovirus to the island
1997	Severe winter, outbreak of moose ticks, new wolf emigrates from Canada

Does this relationship hold after 1995?

Your wording may vary.

No. After 1995, the moose population crashed and remained low due to the severe winter and disease, but the wolf population increased.

A flu vaccine company wants to know which locations are most utilized by adults and children who receive influenza vaccines. Evaluate the graph and use the data to make a prediction as to where the vaccine company should target future sales.

Place of Vaccination for Children and Adults

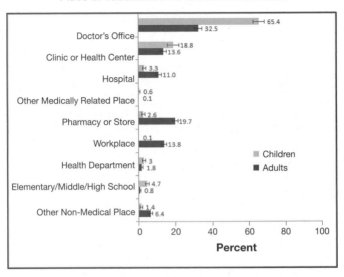

Based on the information in the graph, what are the top three locations where the majority of children get flu vaccinations? Select your answers from the list that follows.

1.	
2.	
3.	

- **Doctor's office**
- **Clinic or health center**
- **Hospital**
- **Pharmacy or store**
- **Workplace**
- **Health department**
- **School**

1.	Doctor's office
2.	Clinic or health center
3.	School

The majority of children get flu vaccinations in doctor's offices, health clinics, and schools.

A flu vaccine company wants to know which locations are most utilized by adults and children who receive influenza vaccines. Evaluate the graph and use the data to make a prediction as to where the vaccine company should target future sales.

Place of Vaccination for Children and Adults

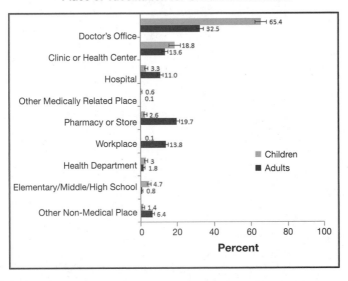

Based on the information in the graph, where do the majority of adults get flu vaccinations? Select your answers from the list that follows.

1.	
2.	
3.	

- **Doctor's office**
- **Clinic or health center**
- **Hospital**
- **Pharmacy or store**
- **Workplace**
- **Health department**
- **School**

1.	Doctor's office
2.	Pharmacy or store
3.	Workplace

A flu vaccine company wants to know which locations are most utilized by adults and children who receive influenza vaccines. Evaluate the graph and use the data to make a prediction as to where the vaccine company should target future sales.

Place of Vaccination for Children and Adults

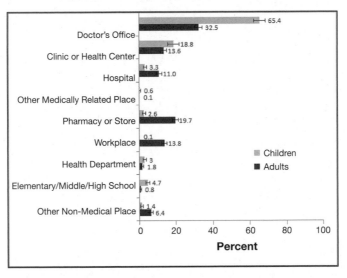

If the flu vaccine company wishes to increase sales to both adults and children, then it should target future sales activities to _____.

· ·

If the flu vaccine company wishes to increase sales to both adults and children, then it should target future sales activities to **doctor's offices**.

In an experiment, Jan records the heights in centimeters of five plants:

$$10.1, 9.8, 10.0, 10.1, 9.9$$

The mean height of the plants is _____ cm.

. . . .

In an experiment, Jan records the heights in centimeters of five plants:

$$10.1, 9.8, 10.0, 10.1, 9.9$$

The median height of the plants is _____ cm.

. . . .

In an experiment, Jan records the heights in centimeters of five plants:

$$10.1, 9.8, 10.0, 10.1, 9.9$$

The mode height of the plants is _____ cm.

The mean height of the plants is **9.98** cm.

The mean is calculated like this:

$$\overline{X} = \frac{10.1 + 9.8 + 10.0 + 10.1 + 9.9}{5}$$

$$\overline{X} = \frac{49.9}{5}$$

$$\overline{X} = 9.98$$

. . . .

The median height of the plants is **10.0** cm.

First arrange the heights in ascending order:

9.8, 9.9, 10.0, 10.1, 10.1

The median is the middle value, which is 10.0 cm.

. . . .

The mode height of the plants is **10.1** cm.

First arrange the heights in ascending order:

9.8, 9.9, 10.0, 10.1, 10.1

The mode is the most frequent value, which is 10.1 cm.

In an experiment, Jan records the heights in centimeters of five plants:

$$10.1, 9.8, 10.0, 10.1, 9.9$$

Next, find the variance and standard deviation of the plant heights. The height values and mean have already been plugged into the table. Fill in the remaining cells in the table with the appropriate values. You may use a calculator.

Values	–	Mean	=	x^2	=
10.1	–	9.98	0.12	___ × ___	___
9.8	–	9.98	–0.18	___ × ___	___
10.0	–	9.98	0.02	___ × ___	___
10.1	–	9.98	0.12	___ × ___	___
9.9	–	9.98	–0.08	___ × ___	___
				Total:	___

· ·

In an experiment, Jan records the heights in centimeters of five plants:

$$10.1, 9.8, 10.0, 10.1, 9.9$$

Now, complete the equation to find the variance using the sum you arrived at in the table in the previous flash card. Remember, n is the number of items in the sample.

$$\sigma_X^2 = \frac{\text{The total from the table goes here}}{n-1}$$

$$\sigma_X^2 = ?$$

· ·

Values	−	Mean	=	x^2	=
10.1	−	9.98	0.12	0.12 × 0.12	0.014
9.8	−	9.98	−0.18	−0.18 × −0.18	0.032
10.0	−	9.98	0.02	0.02 × 0.02	0.0004
10.1	−	9.98	0.12	0.12 × 0.12	0.014
9.9	−	9.98	−0.08	−0.08 × −0.08	0.006
				Total:	0.067

. . . .

$\sigma_X^2 = \frac{0.067}{4}$

$\sigma_X^2 = 0.017$

The variance is 0.017 cm.

. . . .

In an experiment, Jan records the heights in centimeters of five plants:

10.1, 9.8, 10.0, 10.1, 9.9

Get the standard deviation by finding the square root of the variance from the previous flash card:

$\sigma_x = \sqrt{\text{variance}}$

$\sigma_x = ?$

. . . .

$\sigma_x = \sqrt{0.017}$

$\sigma_x = 0.129$, or 0.13

Remember, the standard deviation can be thought of as measuring how far the data values lie from the mean, so take the mean and move one standard deviation in either direction.

The mean of the values was 9.98 cm and the standard deviation is 0.13.

- 9.98 cm – 0.13 cm = 9.85 cm
- 9.98 cm + 0.13 cm = 10.11 cm

Therefore, the height of the population falls within one standard deviation from the mean (i.e., between 9.85 cm and 10.11 cm), except for the plant that is 9.8 cm tall.

. . . .

Refer to the following passage to answer the next five questions.

Hemophilia is a rare bleeding disorder in which the blood does not clot normally. People born with hemophilia have little or no clotting factor, the protein needed for normal blood clotting. It is usually inherited, meaning that the disorder is passed from parents to their offspring through genes. Hemophilia in humans is due to a mutation in a gene found on the X chromosome. Mothers always contribute an X chromosome to their offspring while fathers contribute either an X or a Y chromosome. If hemophilia is found on any of these X chromosomes, it can be passed on to the offspring. A carrier of hemophilia is a female with one normal X chromosome and one X chromosome carrying the mutation. A male cannot be a carrier because his genetic makeup is XY; thus, the presence of the mutation would result in the disease. The chart shown here is a Punnett square that shows the probability of a normal male and a carrier female producing an offspring with hemophilia.

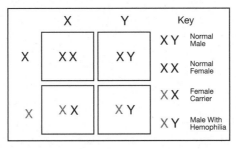

Which piece of evidence from the passage best supports the statement that an affected male will never transmit the hemophilia gene to his sons?
A. **Hemophilia in humans is due to mutation in a gene found on the X chromosome.**
B. **Mothers always contribute an X chromosome to their offspring while fathers contribute either an X or a Y chromosome.**
C. **A carrier of hemophilia is a female with one normal X chromosome and an X chromosome carrying the mutation.**
D. **A male cannot be a carrier because his genetic makeup is XY; thus, the presence of the mutation would result in the disease.**

The correct answer is choice **B**. The statement "Mothers always contribute an X chromosome to their offspring while fathers contribute either an X or a Y chromosome" best supports the notion that an affected male will never transmit the hemophilia gene to his sons because the male does not donate an X chromosome to a son. While the other statements are true, they do not provide the best support.

Which conclusion is best supported by the information in the passage and chart?

A. All the sons of female carriers will have a mutation on the X chromosome.
B. Half of the daughters of males with hemophilia and normal females will be carriers.
C. Female carriers and male hemophiliacs have the greatest risk of having hemophiliac offspring.
D. A female hemophiliac and a male hemophiliac have the highest chance of producing an offspring with hemophilia.

. . . .

The probability of a carrier female and a hemophiliac male producing a non-carrier, non-hemophiliac female offspring is _____%.

. . . .

The correct answer is choice **D**. This conclusion is best supported by evidence in the article because hemophilia is due to a mutation in a gene found on the X chromosome. Additionally, the Punnett square illustrates that females pass an X to sons and daughters and males pass an X to daughters. Therefore, if every X chromosome carried the mutation, every son or daughter would have hemophilia.

· ·

The probability of a carrier female and a hemophiliac male producing a normal female offspring is **0%**.

The Punnett square illustrates that all the possible female outcomes result in the gene showing up, either as a carrier or as a hemophiliac.

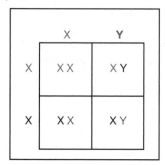

The daughter will be either a carrier or a hemophiliac.

· ·

Which hypothesis can be supported with evidence from the passage and chart?
A. If a female is a carrier, then she can pass the hemophilia gene to a son.
B. If two carriers have children, then they are likely to have children who are carriers.
C. If a male with hemophilia has a son, then the gene cannot be inherited from the mother.
D. If both parents do not carry the hemophilia gene, then potential daughters can only be carriers.

. . . .

The probability of a normal female and a hemophiliac male producing a normal male offspring is _____%.

. . . .

The correct answer is choice **A**. This hypothesis is supported with evidence in the Punnett square and the following excerpt from the passage: "If hemophilia is found on any of these X chromosomes, it can be passed on to the offspring."

. . . .

The probability of a normal female and a hemophiliac male producing a normal male offspring is **100%**. With this scenario, any daughters will have a 100% chance of being a carrier of the gene while sons have a 100% chance of not having hemophilia.

. . . .

Refer to the following passage to answer the next three questions.

A company claims that its new fertilizer, brand X, will make plants, such as tomato plants, grow faster and produce more fruit than a leading brand by another company, brand Y. The directions for each fertilizer indicate that they are used at the same concentration (50 g/kg soil). A scientist uses 150 tomato plant seedlings. He divides the seedlings into three groups of 50 plants. Each seedling is 10–12 cm high at the start of the study and is planted in a pot containing 1 kg of potting soil; the soil is identical for all groups. To one group (control), nothing is added to the soil. To a second group, 50 g of brand Y is added to the soil of each plant. To a third group, 50 g of brand X is added to the soil. All the plants are grouped together in the same greenhouse at a constant temperature of 25°C. The light in the greenhouse is uniformly illuminated and all plants are exposed to a 12-hour on/off cycle. The plants are carefully watered each day with 200 mL of water each. The height of each plant is measured and recorded weekly for 20 weeks. In addition, the amount of tomato fruit produced by each plant is noted at the end of the experiment (week 20).

Effect of Fertilizer on Tomato Plant Production	
Treatment	Average number of tomatoes per plant
Control	3.5
Brand Y	7.2
Brand X	6.1

Did treating the plants with fertilizers increase the fruit production?

· ·

Consider the hypothesis. Did the plants treated with brand X produce more fruit than those treated with brand Y?

· ·

Yes. The fertilizer-treated plants produced about twice as many tomatoes as the control plants.

· ·

No. The plants treated with brand X produced slightly less fruit than those treated with brand Y.

· ·

What would you conclude about the company's claims regarding brand X? Remember that the company claimed brand X causes plants to grow faster *and* produce more fruit than brand Y.

. . . .

Your wording may vary.

The results of this study showed that while the company's claim that plants treated with brand X grow faster may be true, its claim that the plants will produce more fruit than brand Y is not true.

· ·

A student tests the hypothesis that lack of vitamin C will reduce growth in mammals. He takes two mice and puts them in separate cages. One mouse has normal food and the other mouse has food that has no vitamin C. Both mice have the same amounts of water available, the same room temperature, and the same day/night cycles. The student weighs each mouse weekly for two months. The data are shown in the table.

Weeks	Normal Diet (in grams)	Vitamin C-Deficient Diet (in grams)
1	20.0	20.1
2	20.2	20.0
3	20.5	19.9
4	20.3	20.3
5	20.4	20.3
6	20.1	20.4
7	20.0	20.2
8	20.1	20.2

In a lab report, the student concludes that the hypothesis was incorrect. Which statement regarding the student's experiment is true?

A. Measuring the weight of mice was not appropriate to test the hypothesis.
B. The weight of the mouse on the normal diet was not significantly different from that of the mouse on the vitamin C-deficient diet.
C. The experiment had no control.
D. The sample size was insufficient to test the hypothesis.

The correct answer is choice **D**. A single mouse in each group was not sufficient to make a generalization that the hypothesis was true or false.

A survey asks 100 respondents to rate how well they like a particular brand of cereal on a scale of 1 to 4. One (1) represented "Did not like at all," 2 represented "Did not like or dislike," 3 represented "Liked," and 4 represented "Liked very much." The responses were 10, 25, 35, and 30 for responses 1, 2, 3, and 4 respectively. You see that the responses are grouped into distinct categories (1, 2, 3, or 4). So, this is categorical data. One way to visually express this data is to organize it into a table. The first column contains the category of response. This column is usually the independent variable. In contrast, the second column contains the total number of respondents in that category, which is the dependent variable. The table would look like this:

Consumer Opinion of Cereal Brand X	
Response	Number
1. "Did not like at all"	10
2. "Did not like or dislike"	25
3. "Liked"	35
4. "Liked very much"	30

The table allows you to see the data easily. What would you conclude from the data?

The majority of consumers surveyed
A. did not like the cereal at all.
B. did not like or dislike the cereal.
C. liked the cereal.
D. liked the cereal very much.

. . . .

The correct answer is choice **C**. Thirty-five of the 100 consumers surveyed (or 35%) liked the cereal, which was more than any other response.

Inside each cell of your body, ribonucleic acid (RNA) contains information to build proteins. A molecule of ribonucleic acid has four nitrogen bases: adenine (A), guanine (G), cytosine (C), and uracil (U). A sequence of three nitrogen bases makes up a codon, which is a unit that codes for one amino acid.

How many distinct codons can be made from the nitrogen bases of RNA?

. . . .

Suppose a scientist wanted to make an artificial peptide containing five amino acids (there are 20 possible naturally occurring amino acids that she could use). Without repeating any amino acids, how any permutations are there?

. . . .

The molecular biologist wants to make an artificial RNA codon of three nitrogen bases without repeating any single base and the order does not matter. How many possible combinations are there?

GED® TEST SCIENCE FLASH REVIEW

The answer is **64**. There are three nitrogen bases in each codon. Each position can be filled with 1 of 4 nitrogen bases. So, using the fundamental rule of counting, we get:

$$k_1 \cdot k_2 \cdot k_3 = 4 \cdot 4 \cdot 4 = 64$$

. . . .

There are **1,860,480**. For this example, $n = 20$ and $r = 5$. So, here's the calculation:

$$_nP_r = \frac{n!}{(n-r)!}$$

$$_{20}P_5 = \frac{20!}{(20-5)!}$$

$$_{20}P_5 = \frac{20!}{15!}$$

$$_{20}P_5 = \frac{20 \cdot 19 \cdot 18 \cdot 17 \cdot 16 \cdot \cancel{15} \cdot \cancel{14} \cdot \cancel{13} \cdot \cancel{12} \cdot \cancel{11} \cdot \cancel{10} \cdot \cancel{9} \cdot \cancel{8} \cdot \cancel{7} \cdot \cancel{6} \cdot \cancel{5} \cdot \cancel{4} \cdot \cancel{3} \cdot \cancel{2} \cdot \cancel{1}}{\cancel{15} \cdot \cancel{14} \cdot \cancel{13} \cdot \cancel{12} \cdot \cancel{11} \cdot \cancel{10} \cdot \cancel{9} \cdot \cancel{8} \cdot \cancel{7} \cdot \cancel{6} \cdot \cancel{5} \cdot \cancel{4} \cdot \cancel{3} \cdot \cancel{2} \cdot \cancel{1}}$$

$$_{20}P_5 = 20 \cdot 19 \cdot 18 \cdot 17 \cdot 16$$

$$_{20}P_5 = 1,860,480$$

. . . .

The correct answer is **4 combinations**. Here's the solution:

$$_nC_r = \frac{n!}{r!(n-r)!}$$

$$_4C_3 = \frac{4!}{3!(4-3)!}$$

$$_4C_3 = \frac{4!}{(3!)(1!)}$$

$$_4C_3 = \frac{4 \cdot \cancel{3} \cdot \cancel{2} \cdot \cancel{1}}{(\cancel{3} \cdot \cancel{2} \cdot \cancel{1})(1)} = \frac{4}{1} = 4$$

An agricultural scientist conducts 800 trials in crossing pea plants that produce seeds with round seed coats. In these trials, 20 produce seeds with wrinkled seed coats. What is the probability of producing a plant that will yield wrinkled seeds?

. . . .

The probability of having a male offspring is 50%, while the probability of having type O positive blood is 37.4%. The two outcomes are independent of each other.
What is the probability of having a baby boy with type O positive blood?
A. 18.7%
B. 12.6%
C. 87.4%
D. 50%

. . . .

The answer is $\frac{1}{40}$, or 0.025, or **2.5%**. Here's the solution:

$P(A) = \frac{\text{number of trials where A occurs}}{\text{total number of trials}}$

$P(A) = \frac{20}{800} = \frac{1}{40} = 0.025 = 2.5\%$

· ·

The correct answer is choice **A**, **18.7%**.

Here's the solution. Let A represent the outcome of having a male child and B represent the outcome of type O+ blood:

$P(A \text{ and } B) = P(A) \cdot P(B)$

$P(A \text{ and } B) = 0.5 \cdot 0.374$

$P(A \text{ and } B) = 0.1870 = 18.7\%$

· ·

A biologist measures the size of a population over time. The data are shown in the graph.

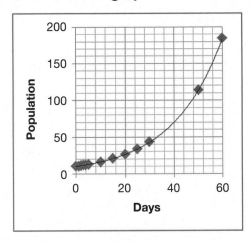

Which statement *best* describes the data?
A. The population is increasing linearly without limits.
B. The population is decreasing exponentially to zero.
C. The population is increasing exponentially without limits.
D. The population is decreasing linearly to zero.

The correct answer is choice **C**. The population is increasing nonlinearly, perhaps exponentially, without limits.

A student reads a lab report on a population growth study. The report contains this graph.

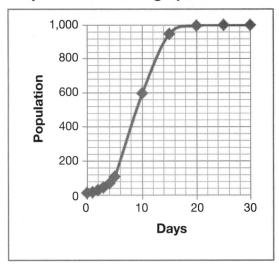

Which *best* describes the model shown in the graph?
A. sigmoidal function
B. linear function
C. exponential function
D. parabolic function

. . . .

In a biology experiment, a student measures the mass of several mice in a control group. The masses (in g) are shown:

19.5, 18.2, 20.1, 20.1, 22.3, 17.9

Which is the median of the data set?

. . . .

The correct answer is choice **A**, **sigmoidal function**. This graph shows a sigmoidal curve, which is characteristic of population growth with limits from the environment.

- -

19.8

Here's the solution. First put the data in order:

17.9, 18.2, 19.5, 20.1, 20.1, 22.3

$$\text{Median} = \frac{19.5 + 20.1}{2}$$

- -

The probability of having a female offspring is 50%, while the probability of having type B negative blood is 1.5%. The two outcomes are independent of each other. What is the probability of having a baby girl with type B negative blood?

A. 0.75%
B. 48.5%
C. 50%
D. 51.5%

. . . .

The diagram shows the difference between an eye with normal vision and one with nearsighted vision.

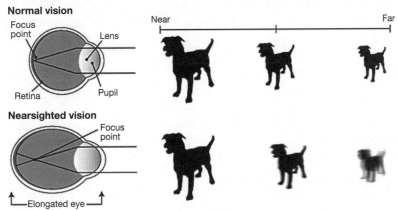

Which part of the eye is best described as a layer at the back of the eye containing light-sensitive cells that trigger nerve impulses to the brain?

A. lens
B. pupil
C. retina
D. focus point

. . . .

The correct answer is choice **A, 0.75%**. Here's the solution. Let A represent the outcome of having a female child and B represent the outcome of type B negative blood:

$P(A$ and $B) = P(A) \cdot P(B)$

$P(A$ and $B) = 0.5 \cdot 0.015$

$P(A$ and $B) = 0.0075 = 0.75\%$

. . . .

The correct answer is choice **C, retina**. The retina is defined as a layer of light-sensitive tissue lining the inner surface of the eye at the back of the eyeball. The cells that are sensitive to light trigger nerve impulses that travel along the optic nerve to the brain, where a visual image is formed.

. . . .

Water moves easily across cell membranes through special protein-lined channels. If the total concentration of all dissolved solutes is not equal on both sides, there will be a net movement of water molecules into or out of the cell. The diagram shows red blood cells in solutions with three different salt concentrations.

Red Blood Cells in Solutions of Different NaCl Concentrations

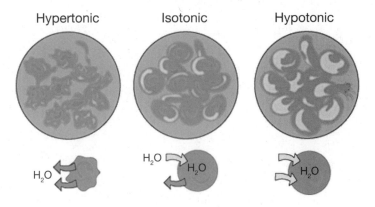

According to this diagram, when will homeostasis occur in red blood cells?
A. when the osmotic pressure of water is equal
B. when the concentration of salt is higher outside the cell
C. when the amount of water inside the cell is higher than outside the cell
D. when the osmotic flow of water out of the cell is greater than salt solution inside the cell

The correct answer is choice **A**, when the osmotic pressure of water is equal. When the osmotic pressure outside the red blood cells is the same as the pressure inside the cells, the solution is isotonic with respect to the cytoplasm. This is the usual condition of red blood cells in plasma in a state of homeostasis.

Refer to the following passage to answer the next three questions.

Tetanus is a non-contagious infection caused by rod-shaped, anaerobic bacteria, *Clostridium tetani*, or *C. tetani*, which affects skeletal muscles by releasing an endotoxin manufactured in the outer portion of the cell wall. The toxin infects the central nervous system and causes prolonged muscle spasms. Infection occurs through contamination of wounds and can be prevented by proper immunization. Most developed countries provide tetanus vaccinations as a standard of health care.

Often, tetanus is associated with rust. Rusting occurs when oxygen, water, and iron interact in a process called oxidation. Over time, the iron mass will convert to iron oxide, or rust. A rusted surface provides a thriving environment for organisms with low-oxygen needs.

Tetanus occurs worldwide, but is most common in hot, damp climates with manure-treated soils. *C. tetani* endospores are widely distributed in the intestines of many animals such as cattle, chickens, and sheep.

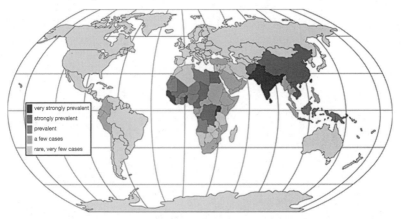

very strongly prevalent
strongly prevalent
prevalent
a few cases
rare, very few cases

Explain how a non-contagious disease, such as tetanus, comes to be so widespread in certain parts of the world. Include multiple pieces of evidence from the text to support your answer.

. . . .

Answers may vary.

It is probable that the countries with the highest incidence of tetanus infection are those least likely to vaccinate while also harboring the most favorable soil and climate conditions for *C. tetani* endospores. Although *C. tetani* thrives on the low-oxygen surfaces of rusted metals, it is most common in the hot, damp climates of equatorial countries. Developed, vaccinating nations, such as the United States, Canada, and Australia, have low or no reported cases of tetanus. However, tetanus is strongly prevalent in third world countries such as India and those found in Africa. Less developed, third world nations are less likely to immunize people; thus, the rates of tetanus infections are strongly prevalent, even though it is not contagious. Toxins from *C. tetani* enter unvaccinated bodies through open wounds, attack the central nervous system, and cause prolonged muscle spasms.

Anaerobic bacteria such as *Clostridium tetani* use the process of fermentation to obtain nutrition. The bacteria use organic compounds, typically found in the intestinal tracts of animals, to ferment sugars for energy, and produce various acids and alcohol by-products.

Identify the correct products in the fermentation equation that follows the list. Fill in each line with the correct term from the list.

- oxygen
- water
- ethanol
- energy

glucose → _____ + carbon dioxide (+ _____ released)

. . . .

The diagram shows some basic components of bacterial cells.

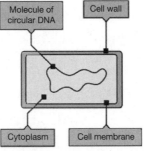

Diagram of bacterial cell

Based on the information in the passage and in the diagram, which cellular component is responsible for both the shape of *Clostridium tetani* and endotoxin production?

A. DNA
B. cell wall
C. cytoplasm
D. cell membrane

. . . .

glucose → **ethanol** + carbon dioxide (+ **energy** released)

The first product is **ethanol**. The phrase "alcohol by-products" clues the choice for the first product. Oxygen is clearly incorrect, as both the preceding paragraph and the passage indicate that the bacteria are anaerobic, and thus cannot use oxygen to respire. Water is a factor in the anaerobic fermentation process in that anaerobes are commonly found and used in waste water treatments, but it is not a component in the simplified fermentation equation.

The second product is **energy**. The statement "the bacteria use organic compounds, typically found in the intestinal tracts of animals, to ferment sugars for energy" indicates that the purpose of fermentation is to create energy to be released.

· ·

The correct answer is **B**, **cell wall**. The cell wall provides rigidity to maintain cell shape. Additionally, endotoxins are produced in the outer portion of the cell wall.

Refer to the following passage to answer the next three questions.

Bufo marinus, commonly referred to as the cane toad, can measure six to nine inches long and weigh up to four pounds. The cane toad is nocturnal, breeds year-round, and releases a toxin from the shoulders that is fatal to vertebrates. It eats crawling insects, small birds, mammals, and other amphibians, including smaller cane toads. It is native to tropical America, but is permanently established in Australia. In the 1930s, sugarcane farmers imported the toads to Australia in attempts to control cane beetles.

Adult cane beetles measure about 13 millimeters long and are black, hard-shelled, dome-shaped flying insects with strong legs. They eat the leaves of sugarcane while their larvae hatch underground and destroy the plant's roots. The flying beetles and burrowing larvae are difficult to eradicate. There is no evidence that the introduced cane toads have had any impact on cane beetle populations. Cane toads have, however, had a significant impact on Australian ecology, including the depletion of native species that die when eating cane toads, the poisoning of humans and their pets, and the decline of native animals preyed upon by the toads. While many populations of native species declined in the decades following the introduction of cane toads, some are now beginning to recover. One species of crow has even learned how to eat cane toads from the underbelly in order to avoid the venom.

Which of the following pieces of evidence supports the theory that the behaviors of other organisms are limiting resources for young cane toads?
A. Adult cane toads often prey on juvenile cane toads.
B. Cane beetle larvae are buried underground and are inaccessible to cane toads.
C. Adult cane beetles have heavy exoskeletons and the ability to fly.
D. Cane toad tadpoles can exist only in aquatic environments.

The correct answer is choice **A**. Adult cane toads often prey on juvenile cane toads. Adult cane toads could be a limiting factor for the juvenile cane toad population because large cane toads prey on other amphibians, even smaller cane toads.

Based on the information in the passage, which of these terms best describes the effect seen in crows that eat cane toads?

A. speciation
B. adaptation
C. development
D. homeostasis

. . . .

Discuss the impact cane toads have had on the Australian ecosystem. Include multiple pieces of evidence from the text to support your answer.

. . . .

The correct answer is choice **B, adaptation**. Adaptation is the evolutionary process whereby an organism becomes better able to live in its habitat or habitats. Over time, the crows learned a way to prey on cane toads without exposing themselves to the toxins released from the cane toad's shoulders.

· ·

Answers may vary.

Cane toads are not native to Australia. They were imported about 80 years ago in an attempt to control the cane beetle, a pest that destroys sugarcane. Cane toads had no significant impact on the flying and burrowing beetle. However, they had a devastating impact on Australian ecology that includes the depletion of certain native species. Many species have been in decline for decades and are only recently beginning to recover.

· ·

Refer to the following passage to answer the next three questions.

In a marine ecosystem, there is a unique relationship between corals and the photosynthetic protists that live on the coral reefs. The single-celled protists, called *zooxanthellae*, live in the tissue of corals and transform large amounts of carbon dioxide into usable energy. The photosynthetic products are used by the corals for metabolic functions or as building blocks in the making of proteins, fats, and carbohydrates.

Although many of a coral's energy needs are supplied by these zooxanthellae, most corals also capture food particles with their stinging tentacles. Prey ranges in size from small fish to microscopic zooplankton. These food sources supply corals and zooxanthellae with nitrogen.

Based on the passage, corals and zooxanthellae demonstrate which type of symbiotic relationship?
A. mutualism
B. parasitism
C. amensalism
D. commensalism

The correct answer is choice **A**, **mutualism**. The unique mutualism between corals and their photosynthetic zooxanthellae is the driving force behind the settlement, growth, and productivity of coral reefs. This mutualistic relationship is beneficial to the zooxanthellae by providing a host and expelled carbon dioxide for photosynthesis. The corals benefit when they use the products of the zooxanthellae's photosynthesis for metabolic functions or as building blocks in the making of proteins, fats, and carbohydrates.

Examine the trophic levels of a marine food web in the diagram. The trophic pyramid groups organisms by the role the organisms play in the food web.

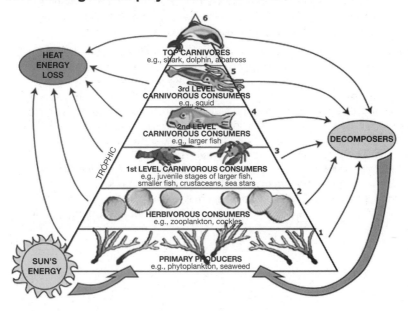

Write the appropriate answers on the lines.

Zooxanthellae are described in the passage as _____.

Based on the trophic levels identified in this pyramid, zooxanthellae would be classified as _____.

Zooxanthellae are described in the passage as **mutualistic photosynthesizers**. Producers are described as autotrophic, which means they are able to make their own food. Just like producers on land, producers in the marine environment convert energy from the sun into food energy through photosynthesis. Phytoplankton are the most abundant and widespread producers in the marine environment.

Based on the trophic levels identified in this pyramid, zooxanthellae would be classified as **primary producers**. Organisms in food webs are commonly divided into trophic levels. These levels can be illustrated in a trophic pyramid, where organisms are grouped by the roles they play in the food web. For example, the first level forms the base of the pyramid and is made up of producers. The second level is made up of herbivorous consumers, and so on. On average, only 10% of the energy from an organism is transferred to its consumer. The rest is lost as waste, movement energy, heat energy, and so on. As a result, each trophic level supports a smaller number of organisms—in other words, it has less biomass. This means that a top-level consumer, such as a shark, is supported by millions of primary producers from the base of the food web or trophic pyramid.

The diagram shows a marine food web.

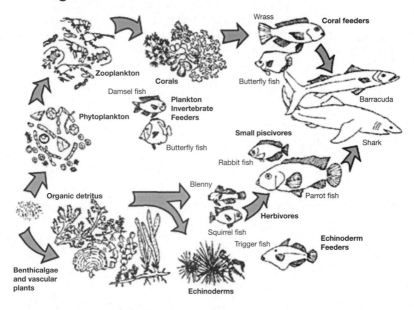

Using the information provided within the passage, identify the organism in the marine food web that supplies coral with energy by circling it.

. . . .

The correct answer is **zooplankton**. The passage states, "Although many of a coral's energy needs are supplied by these zooxanthellae, most corals also capture food particles with their stinging tentacles. Prey ranges in size from small fish to microscopic zooplankton." The marine food web clearly depicts an arrow originating with zooplankton that points toward corals. This indicates that the flow of energy moves from zooplankton into corals.

As seen in the following diagram, living things are highly organized, with specialized structures performing specific functions at every level of organization.

specialized ⟶ tissue ⟶ organ ⟶ system ⟶ organism
cell

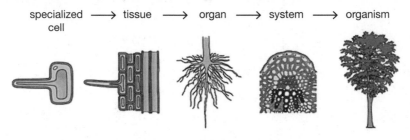

Select the correct sequence of cellular organization. Begin with the most specialized component.
A. red blood cell → blood → heart → cardiovascular system
B. cardiovascular system → heart → blood → red blood cell
C. red blood cell → blood → cardiovascular system → heart
D. heart → cardiovascular system → blood → red blood cell

. . . .

The correct answer is choice **A**: red blood cell → blood → heart → cardiovascular system. The correct sequence moves from most specialized to higher levels of organization.

· ·

The letters shown here show the genotypes of two parents.

$$Yy \times Yy$$

The Punnett square shows the possible combinations of parent alleles. Write the remaining correct combination of the parent alleles in the empty box.

	Y	y
Y	YY	Yy
y	Yy	

. . . .

Probability is an important skill for figuring out answers to GED Science questions. This is an example of a probability question. Five parts of the human body and two diseases are written on scraps of paper and placed into a hat. What is the probability of picking a disease out of the hat?

. . . .

Judy measured the heights of several seedlings that she used in a control group of an experiment. The heights in cm were: 9.9, 10.2, 10.6, 9.3, 10.2, 10.2, 10.0.

What is the mean?

The correct answer is **yy**. In a Punnett square, the alleles combine, one from the side and one from the top, in each box. The two lowercase "y" alleles combine in the bottom right box of the Punnett square, indicating that a recessive phenotype is possible when two heterozygous genotypes combine.

· ·

The event is choosing one of the two diseases rather than one of the five parts of the human body. This is what you want to answer:

1. The number of outcomes is the total number of scraps of paper, 7.

2. There are 2 diseases.

3. $2 \div 7 = 0.2857$

The probability of picking a disease is 29% of the time.

· ·

The mean is **10.1**.

Let's arrange the values in ascending order: 9.3, 9.9, 10.0, 10.2, 10.2, 10.2, 10.6.

The first descriptor is the **mean** $(\overline{X})$ or average. It is calculated by adding up all the values and dividing the sum (Σx) by the number of values (n):

$$\overline{X} = \frac{\sum_{i=}^{n} x_{i.}}{n}$$

$$\overline{X} = \frac{9.3 + 9.9 + 10.0 + 10.2 + 10.2 + 10.2 + 10.6}{7}$$

$$\overline{X} = \frac{70.4}{7}$$

$$\overline{X} = 10.1$$

Judy measured the heights of several seedlings that she used in a control group of an experiment. The heights in cm were: 9.9, 10.2, 10.6, 9.3, 10.2, 10.2, 10.0.

What is the median?

· ·

Judy measured the heights of several seedlings that she used in a control group of an experiment. The heights in cm were: 9.9, 10.2, 10.6, 9.3, 10.2, 10.2, 10.0.

What is the mode?

· ·

What is the endoplasmic reticulum?

The second descriptor is the **median** or middle value. If *n* is an odd number, then the median value is easy to spot. If *n* is an even number, then the median is the average of the center two values. In this example, *n* is odd so the median is easy to spot. The median is **10.2**.

. . . .

The third descriptor is the mode, which is the most frequent value. In this example, there are three values of 10.2 and one each of all the others. Therefore, the mode is **10.2**.

. . . .

An organelle that is used to transport proteins throughout the cell.

What does inorganic mean?

. . . .

What is mitosis?

. . . .

What is meiosis?

A material that is neither plant nor animal in origin.

. . . .

A process of cellular reproduction in which cells produce genetically identical offspring.

. . . .

A process of cellular reproduction where the daughter cells have half the amount of chromosomes. This is used for purposes of sexual reproduction to produce sex cells that will be able to form an offspring with a complete set of chromosomes with different DNA than the parents.

What is a nucleotide?

. . . .

What is phloem?

. . . .

What is protein synthesis?

The smallest unit of DNA. There are five different types of nucleotides: adenine, guanine, thymine, cytosine, and uracil. The arrangement of genes is based directly on the specific arrangement of nucleotides.

. . . .

Vascular tissue found in plants that transports mostly sugar and water; can travel either "shoot to root" or "root to shoot."

. . . .

A process by which DNA will transport its information by way of RNA to the ribosomes where proteins will be assembled.

What are veins?

. . . .

In plants, veins are found in the leaves. They are sometimes called the vascular bundle, which contains the xylem and phloem. In animals, veins are tubelike tissue that usually transports blood.

. . . .

Refer to the following passage to answer the next six questions.

A student is creating a science experiment for the science fair to research whether temperature affects the growth of tadpoles. He collects nine newly born tadpoles and separates them into three groups. He measures the size of each tadpole in each group, places them in equal amounts of water that is changed at the same time for each container, and feeds them equal quantities and types of food. In the first container, he maintains the temperature at 80 degrees. In the second container, he maintains the temperature at 68 degrees. The final container is left at room temperature, which varies around 75 degrees. Just as the tadpoles get to the twelfth week of their life cycle, the student measures the sizes of the tadpoles to determine whether the temperatures affected their overall growth.

What is the hypothesis?

. . . .

What is the independent variable?

. . . .

What is the dependent variable?

That the tadpoles' size will be affected in some form by the temperature of the water.

· ·

The temperature of the water in each container.

· ·

The final measured sizes of the tadpoles.

What were the other variables and were they controlled?

. . . .

Was the number of samples adequate?

. . . .

Overall, was the experimental design appropriate to test the hypothesis?

The food and water quantities were also possible variables but were equal for each container.

· ·

Nine tadpoles was probably not an adequate number for this experiment and the student would have been better able to confirm his hypothesis with more tadpoles.

· ·

The design was appropriate, but the number of samples needed to be increased to confirm the hypothesis.

Which of the following is NOT a physical property?
A. flammability
B. hardness
C. solubility
D. density

. . . .

The smallest unit of matter is
A. a compound
B. an atom
C. a molecule
D. a proton

. . . .

Which is an example of phase change?
A. oil floating in water
B. oxygen diffusing in water
C. paper burning
D. water freezing

Choice **A**, **flammability** is not a physical property. A physical property is something that is observable and measurable and does not involve a chemical reaction. Flammability is a measure of a substance's ability to burn, a property that cannot be determined without chemically altering the substance. For hardness, solubility, and density, each property is observable and measurable.

· ·

Choice **B**, **an atom**, is the smallest unit of matter and is composed of neutrons, protons, and electrons. A compound is made of more than one element. A molecule is made of more than one atom. A proton is part of an atom and not a complete unit of matter.

· ·

Choice **D**, **water freezing**, is a phase change from liquid to solid. Oil floating in water shows a difference in density, not a phase change. When oxygen diffuses in water, it stays as a gas in the water and does not change states. There is no change in state when paper burns. This is an example of a chemical reaction, not a phase change.

Balance the following equation by inserting the correct numbers in the blanks.

____ SnO_2 + ____ H_2 → ____ Sn + ____ H_2O

. . . .

Balance the following equation by inserting the correct numbers in the blanks.

____ KOH + ____ H_3PO_4 → ____ K_3PO_4 + ____ H_2O

. . . .

Balance the following equation by inserting the correct numbers in the blanks.

____ NH_3 + ____ O_2 → ____ NO + ____ H_2O

1 SnO_2 + **2** H_2 → **1** Sn + **2** H_2O

This equation is balanced because there are four atoms of hydrogen (H) on the left and the right of the equation. There are two atoms of oxygen (O) on each side. There is one atom of Sn on each side.

. . . .

3 KOH + **1** H_3PO_4 → **1** K_3PO_4 + **3** H_2O

This equation is balanced because there are three atoms of potassium (K), seven atoms of oxygen (O), six atoms of hydrogen (H), and one atom of phosphorus (P) on each side of the equation.

. . . .

4 NH_3 + **5** O_2 → **4** NO + **6** H_2O

This equation is balanced because there are four atoms of nitrogen (N), 12 atoms of hydrogen (H), and 10 atoms of oxygen on each side of the equation.

Balance the following equation by inserting the correct numbers in the blanks.

____ Fe + ____ Cl_2 = ____ $FeCl_3$

. . . .

All chemical reactions must conserve 1. ____, 2. ____, and 3. ____.

. . . .

If heat is released, the reaction is
A. endothermic.
B. exothermic.
C. equivalent.
E. evaporative.

2 Fe + **3** Cl$_2$ = **2** FeCl$_3$

This equation is balanced because there are 2 iron (Fe) atoms, and 6 chlorine (Cl) atoms on each side of the equation.

· ·

All chemical reactions must conserve **1. matter or mass**, **2. energy**, and **3. electric charge**. Matter can neither be created nor destroyed. The same rule applies for energy and overall charge.

· ·

The correct answer is choice **B**, **exothermic**. Endothermic reactions absorb energy. Equivalent refers to balancing equations, not the heat of a chemical reaction. Evaporate refers to part of the hydrologic cycle, not the heat of a chemical reaction.

What conclusion can be drawn from the chart and caption shown here?

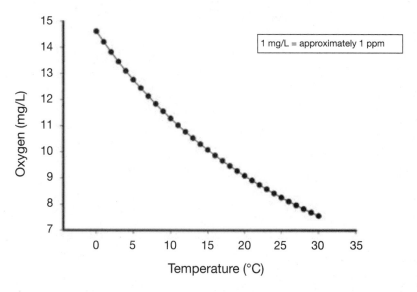

Solubility of Oxygen with Temperature

1 mg/L = approximately 1 ppm

Fish require five to six parts per million (ppm) of dissolved oxygen and cannot live at levels below two ppm.

A. Warmer water holds less oxygen.
B. Fish cannot survive in water at 25°C.
C. As temperature increases, oxygen dissolves more quickly.
D. By doubling water temperature, the amount of dissolved oxygen is decreased by half.

The correct answer is choice **A**. The graph shows that the amount of oxygen dissolved in water decreases as water temperature increases.

The text states that fish can live at two ppm and the graph does not indicate any level lower than seven ppm. The graph does not show the rate at which oxygen dissolves. The graph does not show the relationship of water temperature and dissolving oxygen.

The following image represents sound waves. Label each diagram as low or high frequency.

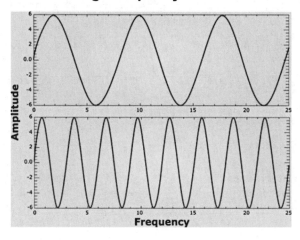

· ·

Calculate the momentum of a 0.25 kg ball that is moving toward home plate at a velocity of 40 m/s.

· ·

Calculate the momentum of a 0.20 kg ball that is moving toward home plate at a velocity of 40 m/s.

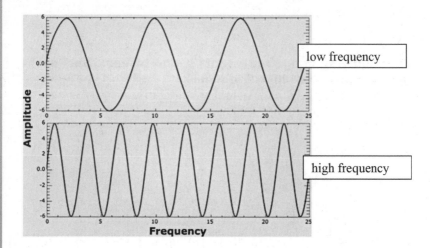

Frequency as it relates to waves is defined as the number of wave cycles that pass in a certain period of time. In sound waves, higher-pitched sounds have a higher frequency. This means that more cycles of waves are compressed into the same period of time. Lower-pitched sounds have lower frequency.

· ·

$p = m \cdot v$

0.25 kg · 40 m/s = **10 kg · m/s**

The formula for momentum is mass multiplied by velocity [$p = m \cdot v$]. The mass of the ball is 0.25 kg times the velocity of 40 m/s.

· ·

$p = m \cdot v$

0.20 kg · 40 m/s = **8 kg · m/s**

The formula for momentum is mass multiplied by velocity [$p = m \cdot v$]. The mass of the ball is 0.20 kg times the velocity of 40 m/s.

Calculate the momentum of a 0.15 kg ball that is moving toward home plate at a velocity of 40 m/s.

· ·

Plot the answers to the next problem on a graph, to represent the relationship between mass and momentum for objects traveling at the same velocity.

Plot the momentum of a 0.25 kg ball, a 0.20 kg ball, and a 0.15 kg ball that are all moving toward home plate at a velocity of 40 m/s.

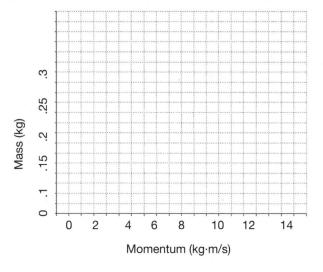

· ·

$p = m \cdot v$

$0.15 \text{ kg} \cdot 40 \text{ m/s} = \textbf{6 kg} \cdot \textbf{m/s}$

The formula for momentum is mass multiplied by velocity [$p = m \cdot v$]. The mass of the ball is 0.15 kg times the velocity of 40 m/s.

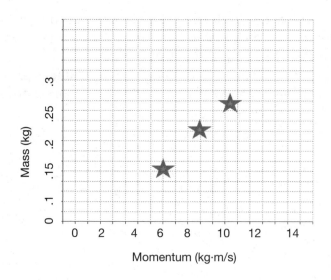

As you can see from the graph, as the mass of the ball increases, the momentum also increases.

What force is needed to lift the 10 kg object with one fixed pulley (assume there is no mechanical advantage)?

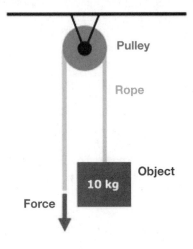

What force is needed to lift the 10 kg object with a two-pulley system (assume there is mechanical advantage)?

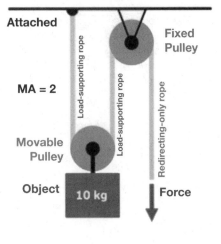

The correct answer is **10 N** of force would be needed to raise the 10 kg object since there is no mechanical advantage. A fixed pulley can make it seem easier to lift an object, but the same amount of force is needed to lift an object with a fixed single pulley as without the pulley (no mechanical advantage).

. . . .

Double pulley system: If you wanted to lift a 10 kg object 10 cm, you would need to apply **five N** of force, reducing the force needed by half. A fixed pulley can make it seem easier to lift an object, but the same amount of force is needed to lift an object with a fixed single pulley as it does without the pulley (no mechanical advantage). Certain types of pulleys do produce a mechanical advantage. The more pulleys that are added to the system, the less force is needed to move the object. The mechanical advantage is increased because the force is distributed over the length of the pulley ropes.

. . . .

If a force of 20 N is applied to a 2 kg object, the object will accelerate at _____ m/s/s.

· ·

If a force of 40 N is applied to a 2 kg object, the object will accelerate at _____ m/s/s.

· ·

A school bus is 20 m long and has a mass of 10,000 kg (10 metric tons) when empty. Determine the weight of the bus in Newtons.

weight = mass × acceleration due to gravity (g)

$g = 9.8 \text{ m/s}^2$

The correct answer is **10 m/s/s**. To find acceleration, you divide force by the mass. 20 N/2 kg = 10 m/s/s.

· ·

The correct answer is **20 m/s/s**. To find acceleration, you divide force by the mass. 40 N/2 kg = 20 m/s/s.

· ·

The answer is **98,000 N**. You calculate the answer by: 10,000 kg × 9.8 m/s^2 = 392,000 N.

When you add 84 passengers (high school students) to the 10,000 kg bus, it can add up to 6,400 kg in additional weight.

Determine the weight of the bus in Newtons.

weight = mass × acceleration due to gravity (g)

$$g = 9.8 \text{ m/s}^2$$

. . . .

A blue whale is 30 m long and has a mass of 40,000 kg (400 metric tons).

Calculate the weight of a blue whale in Newtons

weight = mass × acceleration due to gravity (g)

$$g = 9.8 \text{ m/s}^2$$

. . . .

Acceleration is force divided by mass.

acceleration = force/mass

If a force of 10 N is applied to a 2 kg object, the object will accelerate at _____ m/s².

The answer is **160,720 N**. You calculate the answer by 16,400 kg $\times$ 9.8 m/s^2 = 160,720 N.

· ·

The correct answer is **392,000 N**. 40,000 kg $\times$ 9.8 m/s^2 = 392,000 N.

· ·

The correct answer is **5 m/s^2**. 10N $\div$ 2 kg = 5 m/s^2.

How much force (in Newtons) is needed to raise the object in the pulley system 4?

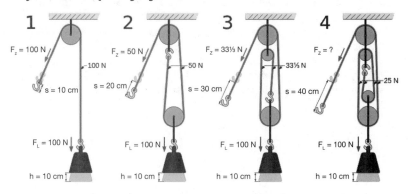

Adapted from Wikimedia: "Pulley diagram with 4 pulleys"

A. 25 N
B. 33 N
C. 50 N
D. 10 N

. . . .

The equation for photosynthesis is:

$$6CO_2 + 6H_2O + Energy \rightarrow C_6H_{12}O_6 + 6O_2$$

Which of the following correctly identify(ies) the reactants in the equation? Choose one or more.

• glucose
• oxygen
• carbon dioxide
• water

. . . .

The correct answer is choice **A, 25N**. The diagrams show the mechanical advantage of using multiple pulleys. There is a proportional relationship between the number of pulleys and the force needed to move an object of constant weight. The force acting on the object is 100 N. With one pulley, there is no mechanical advantage and 100 N of force is required to lift the object. In the second system, there are two pulleys and the force is distributed over the two ropes, so the force needed to lift the object is 50 N. With three pulleys, the force needed is divided by one-third (33.3 N). Finally, with four pulleys the force needed to move the object is one-fourth, or 25 N.

· ·

carbon dioxide, water

Carbon dioxide combines with water in the presence of energy. These reactants produce glucose in addition to oxygen as a waste material.

· ·

Which of the following is NOT true?
A. Atoms can be destroyed in chemical reactions.
B. Matter is composed of atoms.
C. All atoms of any given element are identical.
D. Atoms of different elements have different properties.

· ·

Which of the following statements best describes why a ball eventually slows down after you kick it?
A. An object at rest tends to stay at rest unless a force acts on it.
B. An object in motion tends to stay in motion unless a force acts on it.
C. The amount of momentum an object has depends on its mass and velocity.
D. The strength of the gravitational force depends on the mass of the object.

· ·

Acceleration that is negative is called _____.

Choice **A** is not true. It is the only false statement. Atoms cannot be destroyed in chemical reactions. They can be rearranged and changed, but cannot be created or destroyed.

· ·

The correct answer is choice **B**. The force of friction is acting on the ball to slow it down. An object that is moving continues to move at the same speed in the same direction, unless some force is applied to it to slow it down, to speed it up, or to change its direction. While the other answers are true, they do not explain why the ball slows down.

· ·

An acceleration that is negative (due to an ending velocity that is less than the starting velocity) is called a **deceleration**. For the velocity of motion to change, the speed and/or the direction must change and a net or unbalanced force must be applied. The amount of acceleration or deceleration is directly proportional to the force applied.

This is an image of a section of a roller coaster. What kind of energy is represented at the top of the roller coaster (W)?

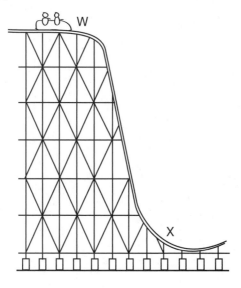

A. kinetic
B. mechanical
C. potential
D. leverage

GED® TEST SCIENCE FLASH REVIEW

The top of the roller coaster represents high **potential** energy, choice **C**.

. . . .

This is an image of a section of a roller coaster. What kind of energy is represented at the bottom of the roller coaster (X)?

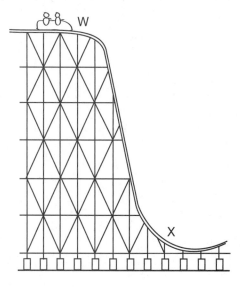

A. kinetic
B. mechanical
C. potential
D. leverage

. . . .

Which of the following is NOT a phase change?
A. wood burning
B. water freezing
C. ice melting
D. water condensing

. . . .

This point (X) shows the point at which the coaster has high energy of movement (choice **A, kinetic** energy).

The bottom of the roller coaster represents high **kinetic** energy, choice **C**.

. . . .

The correct answer is choice **A, wood burning**.

A phase change is a physical process without chemical bonds being formed or broken. In the case of wood burning, chemical bonds are being broken.

. . . .

Fill in the blanks to describe potential and kinetic energy.
_____ energy is energy that is stored. _____ energy is the energy associated with motion.

· ·

The graph shows the solubility of different substances as a function of temperature. What conclusion is NOT true based on the information in the graph?

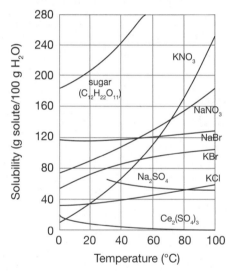

A. The solubility of some substances decreases as water temperature increases.
B. The solubility of sodium bromide (NaBr) is changed very little by increasing the temperature.
C. If you want more sodium nitrate ($NaNO_3$) to dissolve in water, increase the temperature.
D. Increasing the temperature of water will not increase the solubility of sugar ($C_{12}H_{22}O_{11}$) in water.

· ·

Potential energy is energy that is stored. **Kinetic** energy is the energy associated with motion.

. . . .

Choice **D** is not true. In the graph, sugar ($C_{12}H_{22}O_{11}$) becomes more soluble in water as the temperature is increased. The other options are all true based on the information in the graph.

. . . .

The graph shows the density of freshwater as it relates to water temperature.

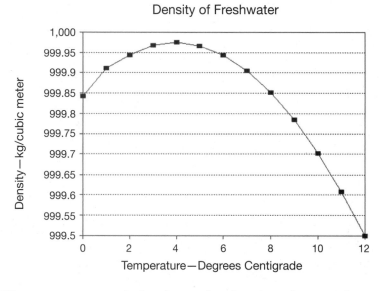

Density of Freshwater

What can you conclude about the density of water from the graph?

A. The density of water increases as temperature increases.
B. The density of water is lowest at the highest temperatures.
C. The density of water decreases as temperature increases.
D. The density of water is highest at the lowest temperatures.

The correct answer is choice **B**. The density of water is lowest at the highest temperatures. The graph shows the density is lowest at 12 degrees centigrade.

· ·

While hiking in a deep canyon, a lost hiker yells out loud. He hears the echo 0.86 seconds after the yell. The speed of the sound wave in the air is 342 m/s. Calculate the distance to the nearest canyon wall.

Here are two formulas that will help.

$$Velocity = distance/time$$

$$Distance = velocity \cdot time$$

HINT: Remember, the echo represents sound traveling to the wall *and* back.

. . . .

Classify each substance as an element, compound, or mixture.

Water (H_2O): _____

Hydrogen (H): _____

Salt (NaCl): _____

Glucose ($C_6H_{12}O_6$): _____

Oxygen (O_2): _____

Saltwater: _____

. . . .

Fill in the blanks in the following sentence using the choices that follow.

Within a system, energy can be _____, but can neither be _____ nor _____.

• created

• transformed

• destroyed

147.06 m

The velocity of the sound is 342 m/s. The time it takes to hear the sound (the time to travel to the wall and back) is 0.86 s.

v = 342 m/s, t = 0.86 s (2-way)

If it takes 0.86 seconds to travel to the canyon wall and back, then it takes 0.43 seconds to travel to the wall.

Now use d = v · t

d = v · t = (342 m/s) · (0.43 s) = 147.06 m

· ·

Water (H_2O): **compound**

Hydrogen (H): **element**

Salt (NaCl): **compound**

Glucose ($C_6H_{12}O_6$): **compound**

Oxygen (O_2): **element**

Saltwater: **mixture**

· ·

Within a system, energy can be **transformed**, but can neither be **created** nor **destroyed**.

Balance the following equation.

_____ $C_6H_{12}O_6$ + _____ O_2 = _____ CO_2 + _____ H_2O

. . . .

Write the formula for glucose, which contains six carbon atoms (C), 12 hydrogen atoms (H), and six oxygen atoms (O).

. . . .

The following illustration shows a solute in a container with a semipermeable membrane.
In which direction will the water move?

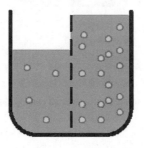

1 $(C_6H_{12}O_6) + \mathbf{6}\ (O_2) = \mathbf{6}\ (CO_2) + \mathbf{6}\ (H_2O)$

This equation is balanced because there are 18 atoms of oxygen on the left of the equation and on the right. There are 6 carbon (C) atoms on each side of the equation. There are 12 hydrogen (H) atoms on each side of the equation.

. . . .

$C_6H_{12}O_6$

Other variations in the order of the formula are allowable, such as $C_6O_6H_{12}$.

. . . .

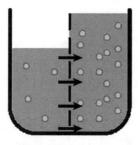

To the right.

The water will move from the area of low solute concentration (in the left section of the diagram) to the area of higher solute concentration (right side of the diagram) until equilibrium is reached.

The movement of water and other types of molecules across membranes (including cell membranes) is important to many life functions in living organisms. Movement of these molecules occurs by diffusion through the membranes, which are semipermeable. These processes, including diffusion and osmosis (the diffusion of water), are sometimes called passive transport since they do not require any energy to occur. The molecules move across the membrane because of osmotic pressure. Osmotic pressure forces highly concentrated molecules to move across a membrane into areas of lower concentration until a balance is reached. This balance is called equilibrium.

Newton's second law of motion is the Law of Acceleration. The calculation can be stated as shown here:

acceleration = force/mass

If a force of 20 N is applied to a 5 kg object, the object will accelerate at _____ m/s/s.

. . . .

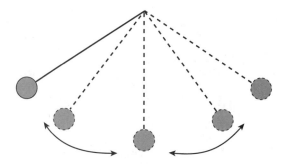

Label these parts of the diagram with Maximum Potential Energy and Maximum Kinetic Energy.

. . . .

Which of the following statements about atoms is NOT true?
A. Matter is composed of atoms.
B. Atoms are created and destroyed in chemical reactions.
C. All atoms of a given element are identical.
D. A given compound always has the same relative number and kind of atoms.

4 m/s/s

20 N/5 kg = 4 m/s/s

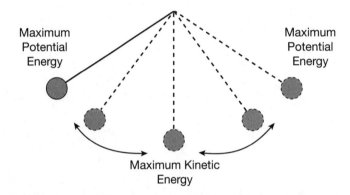

Potential energy is the stored energy, while kinetic energy is associated with motion.

Choice **B** is not true. Atoms are not created and destroyed in chemical reactions.

Match the part of the atom with the correct definition.

1. protons	a. negatively charged particles orbiting around the nucleus
2. neutrons	b. positively charged particles within the nucleus of an atom
3. electrons	c. particles within a nucleus without a positive or negative charge

. . . .

The atomic number of an element is related to the number of protons in the nucleus. Looking at the chart, what can you conclude about the way the elements are organized?

. . . .

What is the difference between ionic and covalent bonds in molecules?

protons—**B.** positively charged particles within the nucleus of an atom

neutrons—**C.** particles within a nucleus without a positive or negative charge

electrons—**A.** negatively charged particles orbiting around the nucleus

. . . .

Elements are organized in order of their proton number, atomic number, and mass.

. . . .

Ionic bonds form when an atom donates one or more electrons to another. **Covalent bonds** form when electrons are shared between atoms.

Place each of the following in its correct state of matter:
- water
- ice
- steam

Solid	Liquid	Gas

. . . .

Place each of the following in its correct state of matter at room temperature:
- diamonds
- perfume
- helium
- vinegar
- metal
- air

Solid	Liquid	Gas

. . . .

Which of the following is NOT a change of state?
A. dew forming
B. gold liquefying
C. boiling water
D. blending fruit

Solid	Liquid	Gas
ice	water	steam

. . . .

Solid	Liquid	Gas
diamonds	perfume	helium
metal	vinegar	air

. . . .

Choice **D, blending fruit**, is not a change of state because blended fruit
is composed of both solid and liquid compounds. In this case, blending is
the chopping of an object until its solid form becomes something similar to
liquid.

What is the measure of how much matter is in an object?

. . . .

How is density described?

. . . .

Assign the following terms to the correct definition:

1. volume	A. the measure of how much a substance will dissolve in another substance
2. elasticity	
3. solubility	B. the measure of how resistant a substance is to shape change when a force is applied
4. hardness	C. the ability of a substance to return to its original shape after deforming force is applied
5. viscosity	D. the measure of a substance's resistance to flow
	E. how much space is occupied by a substance

This is described as **mass**.

· ·

This is the **mass per unit of volume**.

· ·

volume—**E.** how much space is occupied by a substance

elasticity—**C.** the ability of a substance to return to its original shape after deforming force is applied

solubility—**A.** the measure of how much a substance will dissolve in another substance

hardness—**B.** the measure of how resistant a substance is to shape change when a force is applied

viscosity—**D.** the measure of a substance's resistance to flow

What do mass, elasticity, solubility, and viscosity all have in common?

. . . .

Which of the following is a physical property?
A. heat of combustion
B. flammability
C. reactivity
D. boiling point

. . . .

What is the following reaction an example of?

$$2 \, CO + O_2 \rightarrow 2 \, CO_2$$

A. synthesis
B. decomposition
C. single replacement
D. double replacement

They are all **physical properties**.

. . . .

Choice **D, boiling point** is the only physical property. The others are all chemical properties.

. . . .

This is an example of choice **A**, a **synthesis** reaction.

What is the following reaction an example of?

$$CaCO_3 \rightarrow CaO + CO_2$$

A. synthesis
B. decomposition
C. single replacement
D. double replacement

. . . .

What is the following reaction an example of?

$$Zn + 2\ HCl \rightarrow ZnCl_2 + H_2$$

A. synthesis
B. decomposition
C. single replacement
D. double replacement

. . . .

What is the following reaction an example of?

$$AgNO_3 + NaCl \rightarrow AgCl + NaNO_3$$

A. synthesis
B. decomposition
C. single replacement
D. double replacement

This is an example of choice **B**, a **decomposition** reaction.

. . . .

This is an example of choice **C**, a **single replacement** or single displacement reaction.

. . . .

This is an example of choice **D**, a **double replacement** reaction.

What do all chemical reactions conserve? List at least two.

. . . .

What is the difference between an endothermic reaction and an exothermic reaction?

. . . .

Ice melting is an example of which type of reaction?
- **endothermic**
- **exothermic**

All chemical reactions conserve **matter (mass)**, **energy**, and **electrical charge**.

. . . .

An endothermic reaction absorbs heat, whereas an exothermic reaction releases heat.

. . . .

This is an example of an **endothermic** reaction, as the ice is absorbing heat from the surrounding area in order to change its state from a solid to a liquid.

Burning propane is an example of which type of reaction?
- endothermic
- exothermic

. . . .

Cooking an egg is an example of which type of reaction?
- endothermic
- exothermic

. . . .

Condensation is an example of which type of reaction?
- endothermic
- exothermic

This is an example of an **exothermic** reaction, as the burning propane releases heat into the surrounding area in order to change its state from a liquid to a gas.

. . . .

This is an example of an **endothermic** reaction, as the egg is absorbing heat in order to change its state from a liquid to a solid.

. . . .

This is an example of an **exothermic** reaction as the water in gas form is releasing heat in order to change its state from a gas to a liquid.

What is the difference between a homogeneous mixture and a heterogeneous mixture?

· ·

Is seawater a homogeneous or heterogeneous mixture?

· ·

Is smoke a homogeneous or heterogeneous mixture?

A **homogeneous** mixture has the same composition throughout and the components can't be visually separated. A **heterogeneous** mixture has variation in its composition throughout and the components can sometimes be visually separated.

· ·

Seawater is a **homogeneous** mixture. While it is composed of several elements, it is the same composition throughout and cannot be visually separated into its components.

· ·

Smoke is a **heterogeneous** mixture, as it is composed of solids and gas in the form of carbon particles and air.

A uniform mixture is called a _____.

. . . .

_____ is reached when the solution cannot hold additional solute.

. . . .

When playing pool, a cue ball is hit at a stationary eight ball. The cue ball has energy and when it hits the eight ball transfers that energy over. The cue ball then slows down. What is this an example of?

A uniform mixture is called a **solution**.

. . . .

Saturation is reached when the solution cannot hold additional solute.

. . . .

This is an example of the **conservation of energy**.

When sunlight hits a plant and that plant takes the sunlight and uses photosynthesis to grow, that is an example of _____ of energy.

· ·

What type of energy is exhibited by someone jumping rope?
· kinetic
· potential

· ·

What type of energy is exhibited by a child at the top of a slide?
· kinetic
· potential

GED® TEST SCIENCE FLASH REVIEW

When sunlight hits a plant and that plant takes the sunlight and uses photosynthesis to grow, that is an example of **transformation** of energy.

. . . .

This is **kinetic energy**.

. . . .

This is **potential energy**.

What type of energy is exhibited by a fish swimming?
• kinetic
• potential

· ·

What type of energy is exhibited by someone holding a yo-yo?
• kinetic
• potential

· ·

Which of the statements about conduction is NOT true?
• Wood is a great conductor.
• Metal is an excellent conductor.
• A bad conductor is known as an insulator.

This is **kinetic energy**.

· ·

This is **potential energy**.

· ·

Wood is not a great conductor of heat and is instead actually an insulator. This is why we use wooden spoons in boiling pots of water.

What is the word for the reflection of sound waves?

· ·

Which of these statements about waves is true?
A. A ray of light hits a water surface and is both reflected and refracted.
B. Radio waves have the shortest wavelengths.
C. Long wavelengths carry more energy.
D. Electromagnetic waves do not include visible light.

· ·

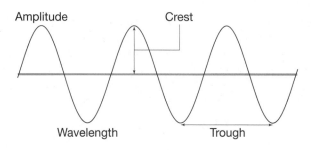

Parts of a Wave

Are the parts of the wave in this diagram labeled correctly?

echoes

. . . .

The correct answer is choice **A**. A ray of light hits a water surface and is both reflected and refracted.

. . . .

No. Amplitude measures height of the crest. The crest is the top of the wave, whereas the trough is the bottom of the wave. Wavelength measures the length of a full wave before it repeats. It's easiest to measure it from trough to trough or crest to crest.

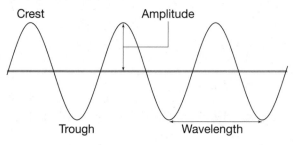

Parts of a Wave

In sound waves, sounds with a higher pitch have a higher
_____.

. . . .

The table shows the maximum amount of oxygen gas that
can be dissolved in water at various temperatures.

Water Temperature (°C)	Maximum Oxygen Solubility (mg/L)
0	14.6
10	11.3
20	9.2
30	7.6
40	6.4
100	0

The data in the table support which of the following
statements about the relationship between water
temperature and oxygen solubility?
A. Bodies of water with a lower average temperature can
   support a higher concentration of dissolved oxygen.
B. Bodies of water with an average temperature higher
   than 40°C contain no dissolved oxygen.
C. A 10°C increase in water temperature results in an
   approximately three mg/L change in oxygen solubility.
D. The oxygen solubility of a body of water is affected by
   many variables, including water temperature.

. . . .

In sound waves, sounds with a higher pitch have a higher **frequency**. This means that more waves are compressed into a period of time.

· ·

The correct answer is choice **A**. The table's data shows the relationship between water temperature and oxygen solubility demonstrating that with water temperature increases, maximum oxygen solubility decreases. This shows that water temperature and dissolved oxygen concentration have an inverse relationship, with highest dissolved oxygen concentrations occurring at the lowest temperatures.

According to the table, bodies of water with an average temperature of 40°C have a maximum oxygen solubility of 6.4 mg/L, and bodies of water with an average temperature of 100°C contain no dissolved oxygen. Temperatures between these two should support oxygen concentrations between 6.4 and 0 mg/L. An increase from 0°C to 10°C results in a 3.3 mg/L increase in oxygen solubility, however, oxygen solubility does not continue to increase by the same increment with each additional 10°C increase in temperature. Also, though many variables can affect oxygen solubility, the table focuses only on the relationship between oxygen solubility and water temperature.

· ·

The table shows the maximum amount of oxygen gas that can be dissolved in water at various temperatures.

Water Temperature (°C)	Maximum Oxygen Solubility (mg/L)
0	14.6
10	11.3
20	9.2
30	7.6
40	6.4
100	0

Researchers find that a body of freshwater with an average temperature of 21°C has a dissolved oxygen concentration of 7.2 mg/L. What is a reasonable prediction of the water's dissolved oxygen concentration after the population size of freshwater grasses doubles?
A. 6.3 mg/L
B. 7.2 mg/L
C. 8.5 mg/L
D. 14.4 mg/L

. . . .

A marathon runner consumes foods with a high carbohydrate content before and during a race to prevent muscle fatigue. This practice, called carb loading, supports which of the following energy transformations within the runner's body?
A. chemical to thermal
B. thermal to kinetic
C. kinetic to thermal
D. chemical to kinetic

. . . .

The correct answer is choice **C**. Grasses release oxygen into the environment as a by-product of photosynthesis. Using this reasoning, it can be predicted that an increase in freshwater grasses will increase the dissolved oxygen concentration. Based on the data in the table, an increase to 8.5 mg/L brings the dissolved oxygen concentration closer to the maximum oxygen solubility for a body of water with an average temperature of 21°C.

Aquatic plants like freshwater grasses release oxygen into the environment. A dissolved oxygen concentration of 6.3 mg/L would result from an event that decreases the amount of dissolved oxygen in the water. A dissolved oxygen concentration of 7.2 mg/L would indicate no change in the ecosystem. A change in the freshwater grass population would alter the amount of dissolved oxygen in the water. A doubling of the freshwater grass population would cause an increase in dissolved oxygen concentration, but not a doubling. According to the table, a dissolved oxygen concentration of 14.4 mg/L far exceeds the maximum oxygen solubility for a body of water with an average temperature of 21°C.

· ·

The correct answer is choice **D**. The runner takes in chemical energy in the form of carbohydrates. This chemical energy is transformed into kinetic energy as the runner's muscles contract and relax, causing the runner to move. Runners carb load to ensure that their body has enough chemical energy to be transformed into the kinetic energy required to run a marathon.

· ·

A highway patrol officer is monitoring the speed of vehicles along a stretch of highway with a speed limit of 55 mph. The results are shown here.

Vehicle 1: 61 mph
Vehicle 2: 48 mph
Vehicle 3: 61 mph
Vehicle 4: 51 mph
Vehicle 5: 59 mph

What is the average speed of the five vehicles? (You may use a calculator to answer this question.)

The average speed can be determined by adding the individual vehicle speeds and dividing by the total number of vehicles. This is calculated as $\frac{61 + 48 + 61 + 51 + 59}{5}$ = **56 mph**.

. . . .

Matter exists in solid, liquid, and gas states. A substance may change between these three states. State changes can alter the physical properties of a substance, as depicted in the following models.

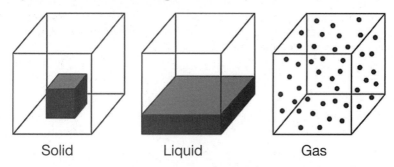

Solid   Liquid   Gas

Which summary best explains the model of the states of matter?

A. Liquids have a fixed shape like solids, but assume the volume of the container like gases.
B. Liquids have a fixed volume and shape, like solids. Gases assume the volume and shape of the container.
C. Liquids have a fixed volume like solids, but assume the shape of the container like gases.
D. Liquids assume the volume and shape of the container, like gases. Solids have a fixed volume and shape.

. . . .

GED® TEST SCIENCE FLASH REVIEW

The correct answer is choice **C**. As shown in the model, a solid has a fixed volume and shape. A liquid has a fixed volume, but assumes the shape of the container. A gas assumes the volume and shape of the container. A liquid has one property in common with solids, and one property in common with gases.

The first summary reverses the properties of liquids. The second falsely states that liquids have fixed shapes. The fourth falsely states that liquids assume the volume of the container.

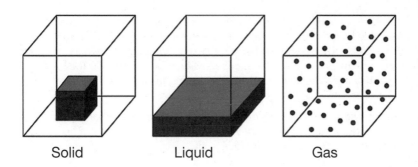

Solid   Liquid   Gas

Based on the model, which state change increases the density of a substance?
A. gas to liquid
B. solid to gas
C. liquid to gas
D. solid to liquid

· ·

The term *exothermic* describes a process in which energy is released, usually as thermal energy. The term *endothermic* describes a process in which thermal energy is absorbed.

Which of the following is an example of an exothermic process?
A. a candle burning
B. a snowbank melting
C. a loaf of bread baking
D. a plant making sugar

· ·

The correct answer is choice **A**, gas to liquid. The density of a substance describes how tightly packed the substance's molecules are. As shown in the model, a substance's molecules are most spread out when in the gas state. This means that a substance's density is lowest when in the gas state. The substance's density increases when going from gas to liquid state because the molecules become more tightly packed.

A substance's molecules become more spread out when changing from solid to liquid state, liquid to gas state, and solid to gas state. This causes the substance's density to decrease.

. . . .

The correct answer is choice **A**, a candle burning. Burning a candle is an exothermic process because thermal energy, or heat, is released as a result of the process.

Melting a snowbank is an endothermic process because the input of heat is required to melt the snow. Baking a loaf of bread is also an endothermic process because the input of heat is required to convert the ingredients to bread. And photosynthesis is an endothermic process because the input of energy (sunlight) is required for plants to make sugar. This means that energy is absorbed during the process, not released.

. . . .

The graph represents the motion of a remote-controlled car. The car's acceleration, or change in velocity, is indicated by the slope of the graph.

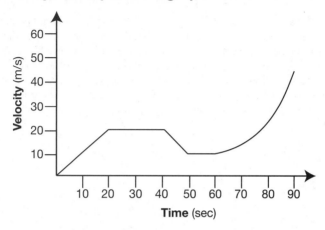

During which time period was the car experiencing a constant positive acceleration?
A. between 0 and 20 seconds
B. between 20 and 40 seconds
C. between 40 and 50 seconds
D. between 50 and 90 seconds

. . . .

The correct answer is choice **A**. The car has a constant positive acceleration when the car's velocity is increasing at a steady, or constant, rate. Between 0 and 20 seconds, the graph moves upward in a straight diagonal line, indicating that the velocity is increasing at a constant rate.

Between 20 and 40 seconds, the car is maintaining a constant velocity of 20 m/s. Since the velocity is constant within this time period, the car is not accelerating (has an acceleration of 0 m/s^2). Between 40 and 50 seconds, the car's velocity is decreasing at a constant rate. This indicates a constant negative acceleration. Between 50 and 90 seconds, the car's velocity is increasing, but not at a constant rate. The graph moves upward in a curved line within this time period, indicating that the velocity is increasing at a variable rate.

The mechanical advantage (MA) of a machine is a measure of how much the machine multiplies the input force applied to it.

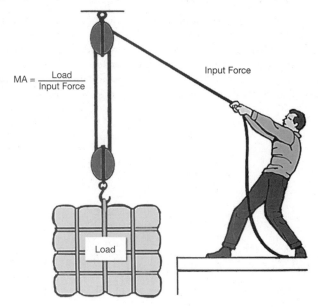

$$MA = \frac{Load}{Input\ Force}$$

Input Force

Load

The table shows the input force required to lift different loads using the pulley system shown in the illustration.

Load (N)	Input Force (N)
30	10
60	20
90	30
150	50

Based on the data in the table, what happens to the mechanical advantage of the pulley system as the load size increases?

A. The mechanical advantage increases at a constant rate.
B. The system's mechanical advantage does not change.
C. The pulley system multiplies the mechanical advantage.
D. The mechanical advantage decreases at a constant rate.

. . . .

The correct answer is choice **B**. The mechanical advantage of a pulley system does not change with the load. Mechanical advantage is calculated as load divided by input force. In the data table, dividing each load by its corresponding input force produces a mechanical advantage of three.

As the load size increases, the input force required to lift the load increases at a constant rate. The mechanical advantage of the pulley system does not change. A pulley system multiplies the input force, not the mechanical advantage, applied to a load. No decrease in mechanical advantage occurs with an increase in load. The mechanical advantage of a pulley system is constant regardless of the size of the load.

The mechanical advantage (MA) of a machine is a measure of how much the machine multiplies the input force applied to it.

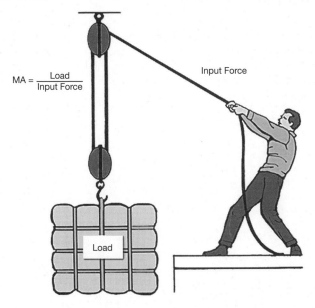

$$MA = \frac{Load}{Input\ Force}$$

Input Force

Load

The table shows the input force required to lift different loads using the pulley system shown in the illustration.

Load (N)	Input Force (N)
30	10
60	20
90	30
150	50

A one Newton load has a mass of 10 grams. According to the table, what is the maximum mass that can be lifted by the pulley system using an input force of 50 Newtons?
A. 15 grams
B. 50 grams
C. 150 grams
D. 1,500 grams

According to the table, an input force of choice **B**, **50 grams** can lift a 150 N load. If a 1 N load has a mass of 10 grams, the mass of a load can be determined by multiplying the force of the load by 10. A 150 N load therefore has a mass of 1,500 grams.

Fifteen grams is the result of dividing the force of the load (150 N) by 10. The mass of the load is determined by multiplying, not dividing, the force of the load by 10; 50 grams is the value of the input force, not the mass of the load; 150 grams is the value of the force of the load in Newtons, not the mass of the load in grams.

What is a catalyst?

. . . .

What is centripetal force?

. . . .

What is a compound?

An agent that changes the rate of a reaction, without itself being altered by the reaction.

· ·

The net force that acts to result in centripetal acceleration. Centripetal force is not an individual force, but the sum of the forces in the radial direction. It is directed toward the center of the circular motion.

· ·

A substance composed of more than one element that has a definite composition and distinct physical and chemical properties. Examples include carbon dioxide, sucrose (table sugar), and serotonin (a human brain chemical).

What is a crystal?

. . . .

What is a decibel?

. . . .

What is density?

A solid in which atoms or molecules have a regular repeated arrangement.

· ·

A unit of measure for the relative intensity of sounds.

· ·

The mass of a substance for a given unit volume. A common unit of density is grams per milliliter (g/ml).

If a person walks forward one mile in 15 minutes, and then back one mile to the starting point, what measurement would be described as 0 miles?

· ·

How can magnitude be defined?

· ·

What is a formula for acceleration?

Displacement compares the ending point to the starting point. If a person were to walk forward one mile in 15 minutes, the displacement would be one mile. If a person were to walk one mile forward and one mile back in half an hour, the distance traveled is two miles, but the **displacement** is zero. Final velocity would be zero and speed would be four miles per hour.

. . . .

Magnitude can be defined as the measure of a standard unit (for example, 30 miles per hour).

. . . .

Velocity divided by elapsed time.

What is a formula for momentum?

. . . .

What is deceleration?

. . . .

momentum = mass × velocity

. . . .

This is a state in which acceleration is calculated to be a negative number.

. . . .

Refer to the following passage to answer the next nine questions.

In the late seventeenth century, Isaac Newton explained light as consisting of particles. But, in the early twentieth century, physicists began explaining light, not as a particle, but rather as a wave. A wave is a periodic oscillation. The shape of a wave starts from a zero level and increases to the highest point or crest. Then, it decreases past zero to its lowest level or trough. From the trough, it rises again to zero. This wave pattern repeats itself over time. The wave has three properties that describe it: amplitude, wavelength, and frequency. Amplitude (A) is the distance from the zero point to the crest of the wave and has the SI unit of meters (m). Wavelength (λ) is the distance from the peak of one wave to the peak of the next wave or the trough of one wave to the trough of the next wave; λ has the SI unit of meters (m). The frequency (ν) is the number of wave cycles per unit of time; the SI unit of frequency is the hertz (Hz). The speed of a wave is the product of the wavelength and the frequency. In the case of a light wave, the speed of light (c) is a constant (3×10^8 m/s) and is described by this formula: $c = \lambda \nu$. The wavelengths of light vary from extremely short gamma rays ($\lambda < 10^{-12}$ m) to very long radio waves ($\lambda > 1$ m).

According to this passage, what is a *wave*?
A. the distance from one peak to the next
B. the highest point
C. a periodic oscillation
D. the distance from the zero point to the highest point

. . . .

According to this passage, what is a *crest*?
A. the distance from one peak to the next
B. the highest point
C. a periodic oscillation
D. the distance from the zero point to the highest point

. . . .

The correct answer is choice **C, a periodic oscillation**. This can be found in the sentence "A wave is a periodic oscillation." The word *is* signals the definition.

. . . .

The correct answer is choice **B, the highest point**. This can be found in the sentence "The shape of a wave starts from a zero level and increases to the highest point or crest." The word *or* signals the definition.

. . . .

According to this passage, what is a *wavelength*?
A. the distance from one peak to the next
B. the highest point
C. a periodic oscillation
D. the distance from the zero point to the highest point

. . . .

According to this passage, what is *amplitude*?
A. the distance from one peak to the next
B. the highest point
C. a periodic oscillation
D. the distance from the zero point to the highest point

. . . .

According to this passage, what does the symbol λ mean?
A. amplitude
B. wavelength
C. frequency
D. speed of light

The correct answer is choice **A, the distance from one peak to the next**. This can be found in the sentence "Wavelength (λ) is the distance from the peak of one wave to the peak of the next wave or the trough of one wave to the trough of the next wave." The word *is* signals the definition.

. . . .

The correct answer is choice **D, the distance from the zero point to the highest point**. This can be found in the sentence "Amplitude (A) is the distance from the zero point to the crest of the wave and has the SI unit of meters (m)." The word *is* signals the definition.

. . . .

The correct answer is choice **B, wavelength**. This can be seen in the sentence "Wavelength (λ) is the distance from the peak."

According to this passage, what does the symbol A mean?
A. amplitude
B. wavelength
C. frequency
D. speed of light

. . . .

According to this passage, what does the symbol ν mean?
A. amplitude
B. wavelength
C. frequency
D. speed of light

. . . .

According to this passage, what does the symbol c mean?
A. amplitude
B. wavelength
C. frequency
D. speed of light

The correct answer is choice **A**, **amplitude**. This can be seen in the sentence "Amplitude (A) is the distance from the zero point to the crest."

. . . .

The correct answer is choice **C**, **frequency**. This can be seen in the sentence "The frequency (v) is the number of wave cycles."

. . . .

The correct answer is choice **D**, **speed of light**. This can be seen in the phrase "the speed of light (c) is a constant."

According to this passage, how would you describe the formula $c = \lambda\nu$?

. . . .

It is in the passage as "The speed of a wave is the product of the wavelength and the frequency."

. . . .

Refer to the following passage to answer the next three questions.

Oxygen is a very corrosive substance and will combine with many other substances or oxidize other substances. A common example is that of a piece of iron left out in the air. Over time, the iron rusts. The rust is a chemical change and can be described by a chemical reaction. Four atoms of solid iron (Fe) combine with three molecules of gaseous oxygen (O_2) from the air to form two molecules of solid iron oxide (Fe_2O_3). The chemical reaction can be written by this chemical equation:

$$4\ Fe\ (s) + 3\ O_2\ (g) \rightarrow 2\ Fe_2O_3\ (s)$$

This class of chemical reaction is called a *combination reaction*.

Using the information presented in the passage, assign each substance's symbol to its name.

Iron	Oxygen	Iron Oxide

- **O_2**
- **Fe_2O_3**
- **Fe**

. . . .

According to this passage, what does the word *oxidize* mean?

. . . .

Iron	Oxygen	Iron Oxide
Fe	O_2	Fe_2O_3

The symbols Fe, O_2, and Fe_2O_3 stand for iron, oxygen, and iron oxide. You can tell that in the parentheses after each substance is mentioned in the fourth sentence, where the chemical reaction is described.

· ·

Note the sentence "Oxygen is a very corrosive substance and will combine with many other substances or oxidize other substances." *Oxidize* means to combine with oxygen.

· ·

According to this passage, what does the phrase _combination reaction_ mean?

. . . .

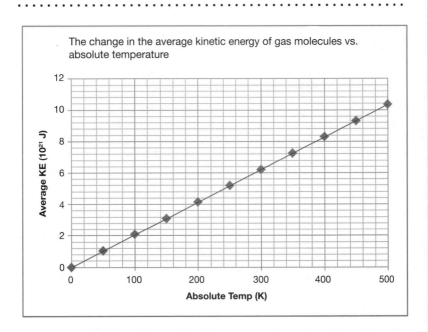

The change in the average kinetic energy of gas molecules vs. absolute temperature

Complete the following statements using the choices that follow.
- In this graph, the numbers on the horizontal (right-to-left), or x-axis, represent the _____.
- In this graph, the numbers on the vertical (down-to-up), or y-axis, represent the _____.
- temperature in degrees Kelvin (K)
- average kinetic energy (KE) of gas molecules

. . . .

A **combination reaction** may be one where molecules combine together to form one product. You can get this from the word *combine* in the fifth sentence, where the chemical reaction is described.

. . . .

In this graph, the numbers on the horizontal (right-to-left), or x-axis, represent the **temperature in degrees Kelvin (K)**.

In this graph, the numbers on the vertical (down-to-up), or y-axis, represent the **average kinetic energy (KE) of gas molecules**.

It's important to note the axis labels. Look at the vertical or y-axis, for example. You see that the numbers are labeled 2, 4, 6, 8, 10, and 12. But if you look at the axis label, each number represents 10^{21} joules (J), not whole numbers. This distinction could be very important if you were asked to answer questions based on the graph.

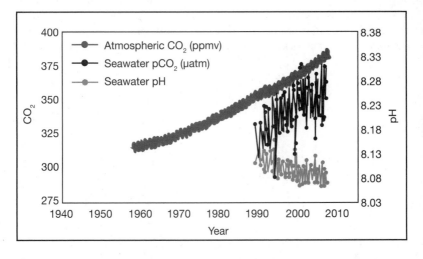

What are the items that are correlated in this graph in your own words?

. . . .

A look at the vertical axes and the legend tells you that this graph shows the correlation between the changes in carbon dioxide (CO_2) levels in the atmosphere and the ocean over time, as well as the pH of seawater over time.

. . . .

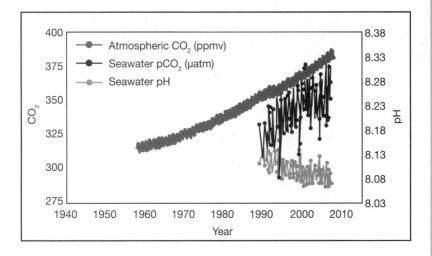

In this graph, which of the following statements is true?

A. As the years passed, atmospheric CO_2 decreased, seawater pCO_2 remained the same, and seawater pH decreased.

B. As the years passed, atmospheric CO_2 increased, seawater pCO_2 decreased, and seawater pH remained the same.

C. As the years passed, atmospheric CO_2 increased, seawater pCO_2 increased, and seawater pH decreased.

D. As the years passed, atmospheric CO_2 decreased, seawater pCO_2 increased, and seawater pH increased.

. . . .

The correct answer is choice **C**. The overall levels of the atmospheric CO_2 and seawater pCO_2 both increased and the seawater pH decreased.

pH		H+ (moles per liter)	H+ (moles per liter)
Acidic	0	10^0	1
	1		
	2	10^{-2}	0.01
	3		
	4	10^{-4}	0.0001
	5		
	6	10^{-6}	0.000001
Neutral	7		
	8	10^{-8}	0.00000001
	9		
	10	10^{-10}	0.0000000001
	11		
	12	10^{-12}	0.000000000001
Basic (or "alkaline")	13		
	14	10^{-14}	0.00000000000001

Look at the pH scale. What is its range?
The pH scale in this chart has values from ___ to ___.

. . . .

GED® TEST SCIENCE FLASH REVIEW

The pH scale in this chart has values from **0** to **14**.

· ·

A chemist measures a solution with a pH value of 9.0. What is the hydrogen ion concentration?

A. 10^{-9} moles per liter
B. 10^{9} moles/liter
C. $\frac{1}{9}$ moles per liter
D. 9.0 moles per liter

The correct answer is choice **A, 10^{-9} moles per liter**. Note that each number on the pH scale corresponds to a negative exponent when the hydrogen ion concentration is expressed in scientific notation. pH 2.0 = 10^{-2} moles per liter, pH 4.0 = 10^{-4} moles per liter, and pH 6.0 = 10^{-6} moles per liter. So, pH 9.0 = 10^{-9} moles per liter.

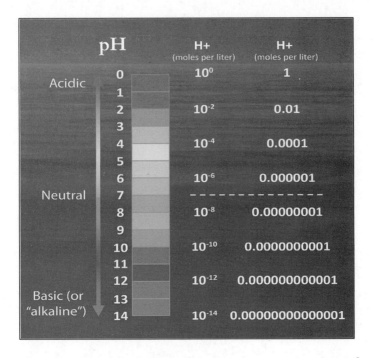

If a chemist measures that a solution has a pH value of 5.5, this indicates the solution is _____.

GED® TEST SCIENCE FLASH REVIEW

If a chemist measures that a solution has a pH value of 5.5, this indicates the solution is **acidic**. Any pH value below 7.0 indicates an acidic substance.

· ·

	pH	H$^+$ (moles per liter)	H$^+$ (moles per liter)
Acidic	0	10^0	1.0
	1		
	2	10^{-2}	0.01
	3		
	4	10^{-4}	0.0001
	5		
	6	10^{-6}	0.000001
Neutral	7		
	8	10^{-8}	0.00000001
	9		
	10	10^{-10}	0.0000000001
	11		
	12	10^{-12}	0.000000000001
	13		
Basic	14	10^{-14}	0.00000000000001

Based on the information in the table, which of these solutions has the greatest concentration of hydrogen ions?
A. pH 2.5
B. pH 4.0
C. pH 7.5
D. pH 10.5

GED® TEST SCIENCE FLASH REVIEW

The correct answer is choice **A, pH 2.5**. Notice that as the pH values increase, the concentration of hydrogen ions decreases (the numbers in the hydrogen ion concentration columns get smaller). So, the lower the pH value, the greater the hydrogen ion concentration. Therefore, pH 2.5 has the highest hydrogen ion concentration of the choices.

Refer to the following passage to answer the next six questions.

A group of students want to know what effect meat tenderizer will have on starches, fats, and proteins.

The group hypothesizes that meat tenderizer will break down proteins, but not starches or fats.

They formulate the following experimental design:

1. Fill six jars with water.
2. Add nine grams of meat tenderizer to three of the jars of water; stir until dissolved.
3. Place one sample of starch, of fat, and of protein in each of the three jars containing meat tenderizer.
4. Place one sample of starch, of fat, and of protein in the three remaining jars.
5. Put lids on all six jars.
6. Observe changes after 24 hours.

What possible sources of errors do you see in this design? Is the hypothesis stated adequately to make a predictable result?

. . . .

Look at the first step of the experimental design. Is there something not specified?

. . . .

What is unclear about step 2? Is there something not specified?

The wording of your response may vary.

In this case, the hypothesis predicts that the meat tenderizer will break down proteins, but not starches or fats. However, what is exactly meant by "break down" is not specified.

. . . .

The wording of your response may vary.

Yes, the size of the jars, as well as the amount of water added, is not specified.

Other things to consider: Are the jars glass or plastic? Do six jars comprise a representative sample of the whole population?

. . . .

The wording of your response may vary.

Although the amount of meat tenderizer is specified, there is no brand or type of meat tenderizer specified. This might be important.

What is unclear about steps 3 and 4? Is there something not specified?

· ·

What is unclear about step 6? Is there something not specified?

· ·

If you were to recreate this experiment at home, do you think it would produce accurate and precise data?

The wording of your response may vary.

Although the directions say to place one sample of starch, fat, and protein in each jar, the amount and types of samples are not specified. What is the source of the starch: bread flour, cornmeal, etc.? What is the source of the fat: butter, lard, vegetable oil, etc.? What is the source of the protein: ground beef, pork, chicken, fish, soybean, etc.?

· ·

The wording of your response may vary.

What type of changes should you look for: changes in size, weight, color, etc.? Under what conditions were the jars kept? Temperature, humidity, and the amount of light are critical variables in many experiments.

· ·

The current design is most likely *not* specific enough to produce accurate data.

Refer to the following passage to answer the next four questions.

A paint company has developed a new brand of outdoor latex paint (brand X) that it thinks might be more durable than another company's brand (brand Y). To save money, the company has employees paint boards of different scrap wood with brand X and brand Y paints. They paint boards with the same number of coats of paint and measure the paint thickness of each board. They place matched boards painted with brand X and brand Y in different environments (desert, temperate forest, arctic tundra) for 12 months. After 12 months, they measure the paint thickness of each board again. They find that the boards painted with brand Y are thinner than those painted with brand X. They conclude that brand X is more durable than brand Y.

What is the hypothesis of this experiment?

If _____ , then _____ .

· ·

Is the hypothesis of this experiment testable?

· ·

The wording of your hypothesis may vary.

If **brand X is more durable than brand Y under outside conditions,** then **the paint thickness of boards painted with brand X will be more than brand Y.**

. . . .

Yes. This hypothesis is testable.

. . . .

Identify the controlled and uncontrolled factors in the experiment.

Place each of the following factors into its correct place in the table.

- The boards were painted with the same number of coats to the same paint thickness.
- The boards were matched in size.
- Weather conditions were varied.
- The boards were exposed to weather conditions for the same amount of time.
- The boards were made of different woods.

Controlled Factors	Uncontrolled Factors

· ·

Name three ways this experiment could be improved.

· ·

Controlled Factors	Uncontrolled Factors
The boards were painted with the same number of coats to the same paint thickness.	Weather conditions were varied.
The boards were matched in size.	The boards were made of different woods.
The boards were exposed to weather conditions for the same amount of time.	

· ·

The wording of your response may vary.

1. All the boards could be made of the same type of wood.

2. Rather than paint separate boards, half of each board could be painted with each brand of paint.

3. The environmental conditions could be more rigorously controlled in artificial ovens and freezers.

· ·

Refer to the following passage to answer the next three questions.

When applying the brakes in a moving car, the force of friction between the road surface and the vehicle tires is what stops the car. The force of friction depends on the coefficient of friction, which varies with the road conditions (dry, wet, icy) and seasons (summer, winter). In an accident, a police officer can measure the braking distance by the skid marks, note the road conditions, and determine the initial velocity of the car. The data are shown in the graph.

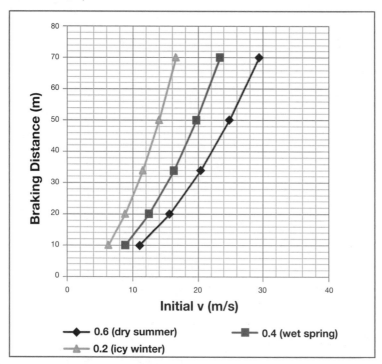

On a road under wet spring conditions, a car has a braking distance of 40 m. The initial speed of the car was _____ m/s.

. . . .

On a road under wet spring conditions, a car has a braking distance of 40 m. The initial speed of the car was **18** m/s.

First, use a ruler to trace a horizontal line from 40 m on the y-axis until it meets the curve for wet spring conditions. From that point, trace a perpendicular line to the x-axis and read the initial speed, which is 18 m/s.

On a road under icy winter conditions, a car is traveling at 10 m/s initially when it brakes. The car will travel _____ m before it stops.

. . . .

On a road under wet summer conditions, a car has a braking distance of 60 m. How fast was the car going initially?
A. less than 15 m/s
B. 15–22 m/s
C. 22–27 m/s
D. greater than 27 m/s

. . . .

On a road under icy winter conditions, a car is traveling at 10 m/s initially when it brakes. The car will travel **25** m before it stops.

First, use a ruler to trace a vertical line from 10 m/s on the x-axis until it meets the curve for icy winter conditions. From that point, trace a horizontal line to the y-axis and read the braking distance, which is 25 meters.

· ·

The correct answer is choice **C**. There is no curve for wet summer conditions, but these conditions must fall between the curves for wet spring and dry summer. Use a ruler to trace a horizontal line from 60 m on the y-axis until it meets the curve for wet spring conditions. This is the minimum speed. From that point, trace a perpendicular line to the x-axis and read the initial speed, which is 22 m/s. Repeat the process, but continue the horizontal line until it reaches the dry summer curve. This is the maximum speed. From that point, trace a perpendicular line to the x-axis and read the initial speed, which is 27 m/s. So, the car had to be traveling between 22 m/s and 27 m/s.

· ·

Refer to the following passage to answer the next four questions.

The Haber process is a chemical reaction where nitrogen and hydrogen gases are combined to form ammonia gas. The reaction is represented by this chemical equation:

$$N_2 \text{ (g)} + 3 \text{ H}_2 \text{ (g)} \underset{\text{endothermic}}{\overset{\text{exothermic}}{\rightleftharpoons}} 2 \text{ NH}_3 \text{ (g)}$$

Chemists studied the effects of increasing pressure on the gases in the reaction. The same amounts of nitrogen and hydrogen gases were combined in a fixed chamber. They increased the pressure of the chamber from 0 to 400 atmospheres (atm). They repeated the experiment at several fixed temperatures from 350°C to 550°C. In each case, they measured the percent yield of ammonia produced in the reaction. The data are shown in the graph:

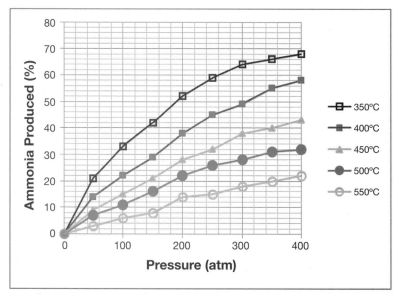

Suppose that you are a chemical engineer and must make a facility that will produce large amounts of ammonia using the Haber process. What would be the best conditions to produce the greatest percent yield of ammonia?

_____ atm at _____°C

400 atm at **350**°C

The best conditions to produce the greatest percent yield of ammonia would be 400 atm at 350°C. These conditions have the highest yield of ammonia (68%).

Which is the highest pressure at which the reaction can be run while still guaranteeing a less than 55% ammonia yield?
A. 100 atm
B. 200 atm
C. 300 atm
D. 400 atm

. . . .

Which is the highest temperature at which the reaction can be run while still guaranteeing a lower than 26% ammonia yield?
A. 350°C
B. 400°C
C. 500°C
D. 550°C

. . . .

When considering ammonia production, what are the best conditions at which to run the Haber reaction?

_____ atm at ____°C

The correct answer is choice **B, 200 atm**.

· ·

The correct answer is choice **D, 550°C**.

· ·

400 atm at **350**°C

In a chemical reaction, the chemist follows the concentrations of four substances (A–D) over time. The data are shown in the graph.

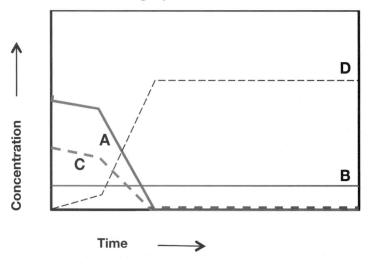

Which chemical reaction is the proper conclusion from the data?

A. $A + B \rightarrow C + D$
B. $B + D \rightarrow A + C$
C. $A + C \rightarrow D$
D. $C + D \rightarrow A$

The correct answer is choice **C**. The concentrations of A and C decrease with time in the same manner, so they are reactants. The concentration of D increases with time, so it is a product.

A student drops a ball from a tall building, while another student videotapes the ball's path. They repeat the experiment 10 times. From the videotape, they measure the distance and calculate the velocities and accelerations with time. They average the values and plot them on graphs shown here.

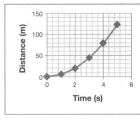

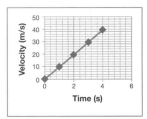

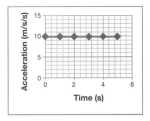

Which conclusions about the ball's motion are true?
A. The velocity is constant, the acceleration decreases, and the distance increases.
B. Acceleration is constant, while velocity and distance increase.
C. The distance is constant, the velocity decreases, and the acceleration increases.
D. Acceleration is constant, distance increases, but the velocity decreases.

The correct answer is choice **B**. The acceleration of a falling object is constant, while velocity increases linearly, and distance increases with the time squared.

A student drops a ball from a tall building, while another student videotapes the ball's path. They repeat the experiment 10 times. From the videotape, they measure the distance and calculate the velocities and accelerations with time. They average the values and plot them on graphs.

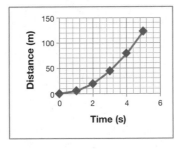

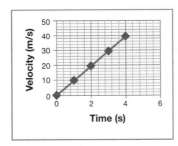

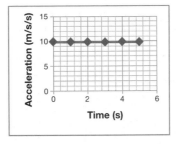

What is one way to simplify the description of the results of this experiment?

. . . .

One way to simplify the presentation might be to eliminate the acceleration graph and verbally state the result:

Acceleration of the ball was constant at 10 m/s/s.

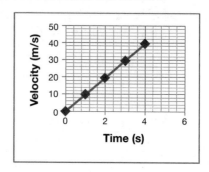

Alternatively, the velocity graph could be described verbally. For example, the velocity of the ball increased linearly from zero at a constant rate of 10 m/s.

Note: The rate of a linear graph is the slope of the line.

Pick any two points on the line and use the slope formula. For example, use (4,40) and (0,0). The slope becomes:

$$m = \frac{(y_2 - y_1)}{(x_2 - x_1)}$$
$$m = \frac{(40 - 0)}{(4 - 0)}$$
$$m = \frac{40}{4}$$
$$m = 10$$

The acceleration of the ball was constant at 10 m/s/s. So, the only graph that needs to be displayed is the graph of distance versus time.

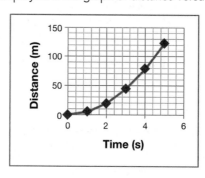

An audit of four preschools in a district shows the number of students and the student-related educational expenses. The data are shown in the table.

School	Number of Students	Expenses
A	20	$ 10,000
B	35	$ 70,000
C	50	$150,000
D	100	$200,000

Which school has the greatest expenditure per student?
A. school C
B. school B
C. school A
D. school D

. . . .

Which set of data supports the hypothesis that force on a spring (*F*) increases non-linearly with the displacement from zero (*x*)?

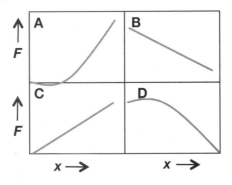

A. set A
B. set B
C. set C
D. set D

. . . .

The correct answer is choice **A**. School C spends $3,000 per student, which is more than the others.

. . . .

The correct answer is choice **A**. This data indicates that force increases non-linearly with displacement.

. . . .

Refer to the following passage to answer the next five questions.

Consider an example of continuous data. Jamie is doing an experiment in physics class. In the experiment, he is trying to answer the question, "How does the velocity of a ball rolling down a ramp change with time?"

Distances along the ramp are marked at 0.1, 0.2, 0.3, 0.4, and 0.5 m. He rolls a ball down the ramp. He starts a stopwatch when he releases the ball at the top of the ramp and stops it when it passes the first mark. He repeats this four times and records the average time. He repeats the experiment again, but this time, he stops the watch at the second mark and records the time. He continues with the procedure until he reaches the last mark. He then records the average times and calculates the velocities. The data are shown in the table.

Distance (m)	Time (s)	Velocity (m/s)
0	0	0
0.1	0.20	0.50
0.2	0.28	0.70
0.3	0.35	0.88
0.4	0.40	1.00
0.5	0.45	1.13

Using the graph, plot points for distance following the data given in the table.

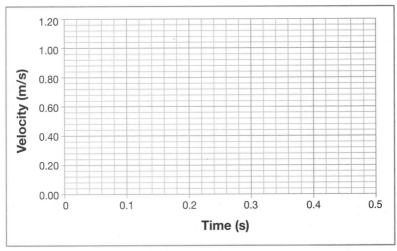

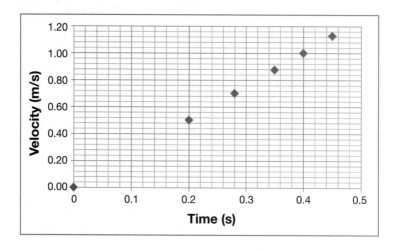

What pattern do the data points make on the graph?

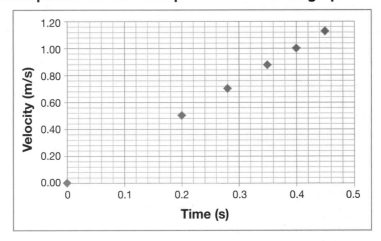

What can Jamie conclude about how the velocity of the rolling ball changes?

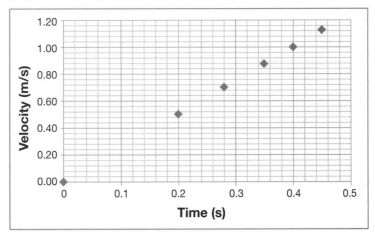

The data points seem to form a line. Draw a line that fits through the data points. It should look like this.

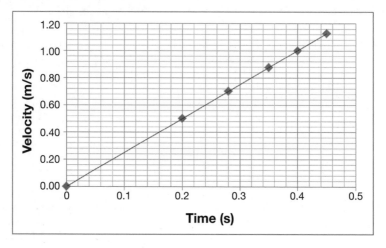

This is called a line graph.

. . . .

As time increases, so does the velocity of the ball. Furthermore, the increase forms a straight line (linear), which means it occurs at a constant rate.

. . . .

Which is the independent variable?

. . . .

Which is the dependent variable?

. . . .

Time is the independent variable. Ask yourself—does the velocity of the ball change time? No. Therefore, time must be the independent variable.

· ·

If the velocity of the ball does not change time, then time may change the velocity of the ball. Therefore, the **velocity** of the ball is the dependent variable.

· ·

Cindy is conducting an experiment on human hearing and musical notes. She blindfolds a subject and plays a reference note like middle C (C_4). Next, she plays another note and asks the subject whether the note was higher or lower relative to the reference note. She indicates a higher pitch with one or more plus signs and a lower note with one or more minus signs. She organizes her subject's responses in a table like this:

Musical Note	Relative Pitch
G_3	– –
A_3	–
Middle C (C_4)	0
D_4	+
E_4	++

Using the following data, what is the proper order from lowest note to the highest note?

- A_3
- C_4
- D_4
- E_4
- G_3

Lowest ____, ____, ____, ____, ____ Highest

. . . .

Lowest **G$_3$, A$_3$, C$_4$, D$_4$, E$_4$** Highest

We can also represent the order with mathematical signs such as $G_3 < A_3 < C_4 < D_4 < E_4$.

· ·

Cindy is conducting an experiment on human hearing and musical notes. She blindfolds a subject and plays a reference note like middle C (C_4). Next, she plays another note and asks the subject whether the note was higher or lower relative to the reference note. She indicates a higher pitch with one or more plus signs and a lower note with one or more minus signs. She organizes her subject's responses in a table like this:

Musical Note	Relative Pitch
G_3	– –
A_3	–
Middle C (C_4)	0
D_4	+
E_4	++

Do we know how much higher musical note E_4 is than musical note G_3, and how do we know this?

. . . .

Jill is watching the development of red color in a solution with time during a chemical reaction. She notes the time and rates the color on a scale of 1 to 10 with 1 being light red (almost pink) and 10 being dark red (almost purple). She expresses her data in a table.

Time (minutes)	Relative Red Color
1	1
2	3
3	5
4	6
5	6

After 1 minute, what color is the solution?

. . . .

Answers may vary.

No, all we know is the relative pitch. This is a drawback to qualitative data.

· ·

The solution is **light red**, (almost **pink**).

· ·

Jill is watching the development of red color in a solution with time during a chemical reaction. She notes the time and rates the color on a scale of 1 to 10 with 1 being light red (almost pink) and 10 being dark red (almost purple). She expresses her data in a table.

Time (minutes)	Relative Red Color
1	1
2	3
3	5
4	6
5	6

Which color does the solution finally develop into?
- almost pink
- red
- almost purple

red

The solution develops a red, perhaps slightly dark red color, as indicated by the middle number of the scale (5 or 6).

· ·

A biochemist conducts an experiment in which she measures the rate of a reaction as a function of temperature. The reaction is conducted in the presence and absence of an enzyme. She also monitors the pH of the reaction. Here are the data:

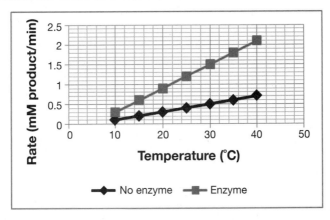

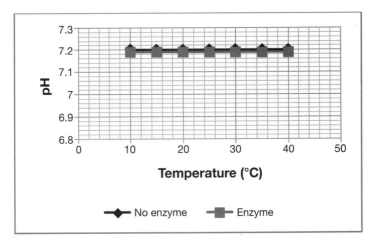

Which data are more important?
- **rate versus temperature**
- **pH versus temperature**

rate versus temperature

The biochemist would want to show the rate versus temperature data, as that is what is changing.

A biochemist conducts an experiment in which she measures the rate of a reaction as a function of temperature. The reaction is conducted in the presence and absence of an enzyme. She also monitors the pH of the reaction. Here are the data:

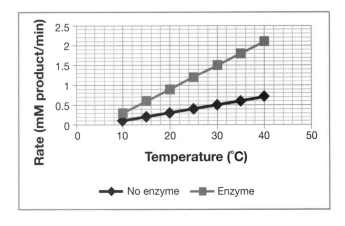

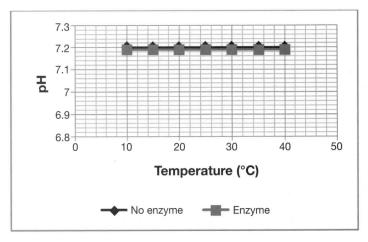

How would you simplify this presentation?

. . . .

Answers may vary.

The pH of the reaction does not significantly change with temperature, and could be easily stated verbally as the pH of the reaction mixture was constant at approximately 7.20.

The graph describes the change in motion of a car.

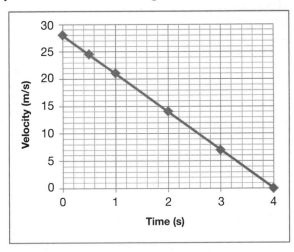

Which statement describes the results?
A. The velocity increases linearly at a rate of seven m/s/s.
B. The velocity increases non-linearly at a rate of seven m/s/s.
C. The velocity decreases non-linearly at a rate of seven m/s/s.
D. The velocity decreases linearly at a rate of seven m/s/s.

. . . .

The correct answer is choice **D**. The velocity is decreasing linearly at a constant rate of seven m/s/s.

A student observes a chemical reaction in a series of tubes. After five minutes of reaction time, she rates the development of blue color on a scale of 1 to 5 (1 = pale blue, 5 = navy blue). The results are shown in the table.

Tube Number	Relative Color
A	5
B	2
C	1
D	4
E	3

Which represents the series of tubes in order from least color development to most color development?
A. A < B < C < D < E
B. C < B < E < D < A
C. E < D < A < B < C
D. E < D < C < B < A

. . . .

The correct answer is choice **B**. The tubes are in the correct order from least color development (Tube C = 1) to most color development (Tube A = 5).

In a physics lab, a student heats an iron block. He measures the temperature change and mass of the block as it heats up. He calculates the thermal energy transferred to the block. The results are shown in the following graphs.

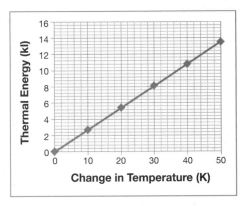

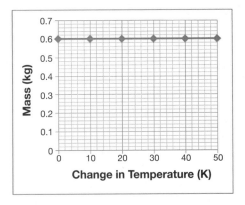

Which best describes the experimental results in words?
A. The thermal energy decreases at a constant rate, while the mass stays constant.
B. The thermal energy increases at a constant rate, while the mass stays constant.
C. The thermal energy decreases at a constant rate, while the mass increases.
D. The thermal energy increases at a constant rate, while the mass decreases.

The correct answer is choice **B**. Thermal energy increases linearly (constant rate), while mass remains constant.

Jenny does an experiment with her friend to test her friend's ability to hear loud (indicated by positives) or soft (indicated by negatives) sounds relative to a reference sound. The data are shown in the table.

Sound	Relative Intensity
A	++
B	--
C	-
D	+++
E	---

Which sound was closest to the reference sound?

· ·

Which graph can be described as decreasing force (*F*) as a non-linear function of displacement (*x*)?

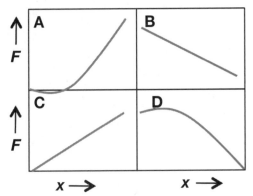

A. graph A
B. graph B
C. graph C
D. graph D

· ·

Sound C had only one negative and was the closest to the reference sound.

· ·

Graph D. This data indicates that force decreases non-linearly with displacement.

· ·

A man is 2.0 m away from you. He walks in a straight line away from you at a constant velocity. His position with time is shown in the table and the graph. What is the man's velocity?

Time (s)	Position (m)
0	2.00
1	3.50
2	5.00
3	6.50
4	8.00
5	9.50
6	11.00
7	12.50
8	14.00
9	15.50
10	17.00

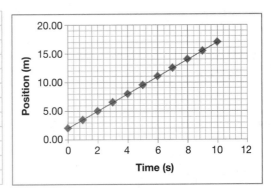

. . . .

A man is 2.0 m away from you. He walks in a straight line away from you at a constant velocity. His position with time is shown in the table and the graph.

Time (s)	Position (m)
0	2.00
1	3.50
2	5.00
3	6.50
4	8.00
5	9.50
6	11.00
7	12.50
8	14.00
9	15.50
10	17.00

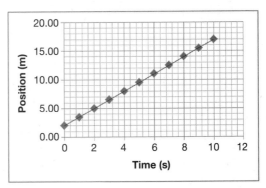

How far away will the man be at 30 s if he keeps walking at the same velocity?

. . . .

By definition, **velocity** is the rate of change of position with time or the slope of the straight line on a position–time graph. It's a straight line because he is walking at constant velocity. So, to find the equation of the line, we must first calculate the slope of the line:

1. Pick any two points on the line. We'll use (2,5) and (4,8).

2. Use the slope equation:

   $$m = \frac{(y_2 - y_1)}{(x_2 - x_1)}$$
   $$m = \frac{(8\text{ m} - 5\text{ m})}{(4\text{ s} - 2\text{ s})}$$
   $$m = \frac{3\text{ m}}{2\text{ s}}$$
   $$m = 1.5\frac{\text{m}}{\text{s}}$$

   So, the man's velocity is 1.5 m/s.

3. Now, let's find the y-intercept. At time zero, the man started from 2 m away. Therefore, the y-intercept is 2 m. You can see this on the graph as well. It's the point where the line crosses the y-axis (vertical axis).

4. So, the equation of the line in the form $y = mx + b$ becomes:
   $y = 1.5x + 2$.

. . . .

47 m. Determine the velocity of the man using the slope equation using two points like (2,5) and (4,8).

$$m = \frac{(y_2 - y_1)}{(x_2 - x_1)}$$
$$m = \frac{(8\text{ m} - 5\text{ m})}{(4\text{ s} - 2\text{ s})}$$
$$m = \frac{3\text{ m}}{2\text{ s}}$$
$$m = 1.5\frac{\text{m}}{\text{s}}$$

So, the man's velocity is 1.5 m/s.

The time is 30 s, so $x = 30$. Use the equation:

$y = mx + b$

$y = (1.5\frac{\text{m}}{\cancel{s}})(30\ \cancel{s}) + (2\text{ m})$

$y = 45\text{ m} + 2\text{ m}$

$y = 47\text{ m}$

A student is following a chemical assay to measure the amount of protein in a sample. The reaction turns blue in the presence of protein. She runs known solutions of protein plus an unknown and measures the amount of blue color or absorbance in a device called a spectrophotometer. The results are shown in the table and graph.

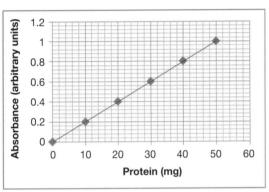

Protein (µg)	Absorbance
0	0
10	0.2
20	0.4
30	0.6
40	0.8
50	1
unknown	0.7

The line formed by the data from the protein standards is called a standard curve.

What is the equation of the standard curve?

· ·

y = 0.02x. The equation of the standard curve is $y = 0.02x$. Here's the solution. Use two points on the line, like (30,0.6) and (10,0.2), and find the slope:

$$m = \frac{(y_2 - y_1)}{(x_2 - x_1)}$$

$$m = \frac{(0.6 - 0.2)}{(30 \, \mu g - 10 \, \mu g)}$$

$$m = \frac{0.4}{20 \, \mu g}$$

$$m = 0.2 \, \mu g^{-1}$$

The y-intercept is zero, so the equation for the standard curve is $y = 0.02x$.

A student is following a chemical assay to measure the amount of protein in a sample. The reaction turns blue in the presence of protein. She runs known solutions of protein plus an unknown and measures the amount of blue color or absorbance in a device called a spectrophotometer. The results are shown in the table and graph.

Protein (µg)	Absorbance
0	0
10	0.2
20	0.4
30	0.6
40	0.8
50	1
unknown	0.7

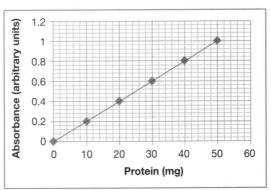

The line formed by the data from the protein standards is called a standard curve.

How much protein is in the unknown sample?

_____ µg

35 µg. There is 35 µg of protein in the unknown sample. You have the y-value of 0.7, so solve the equation for x:

$y = 0.02x$

$x = \frac{y}{0.02}$

$x = \frac{0.7}{0.2 \, µg^{-1}}$

$x = 35 \, µg$

A sound wave has a frequency of 262 Hz. It travels at 340 m/s. What is the wavelength of the sound wave? (If you do not remember the formula, it is $v = f\lambda$ where v is velocity, f is frequency, and λ is the wavelength.)

. . . .

1.30 m. The answer is 1.30 m. Here's the solution (remember that the unit Hz is cycles per second or s⁻¹):

Given: $f = 262$ Hz, $v = 340$ m/s

Unknown: $\lambda = ?$

$v = f\lambda$ Rearrange to find λ.

$\lambda = \frac{v}{f}$

$\lambda = \frac{340 \text{ m/s}}{262 \text{ Hz}} = [\frac{340 \text{ m/s}}{262 \text{ s}^{-1}} = \frac{340 \text{ m/s} \cdot s}{262}]$ This part is shown to illustrate how the units work out.

$\lambda = 1.30$ m

Review the answer. Does it make sense?

Yes, the answer makes sense. The unit is correct and sound waves are rather large (i.e., on the order of meters long).

· ·

Refer to the following passage to answer the next four questions.

A worker on an assembly line in a chocolate factory samples 10 candy bars every hour to make sure that the candy bars produced meet specifications. The specifications of the candy bars state that the candy bar length must be 15 cm ± 0.5 cm. The worker obtains this data set:

15.1, 14.9, 15.0, 14.6, 15.0, 15.0, 15.0, 14.9, 15.4, 14.9

What is the mean of the sample data set?

. . . .

What is the median of the sample data set?

. . . .

What is the mode of the sample data set?

14.98 cm. The mean is 14.98 cm, the median is 15.0 cm, and the mode is 15.0 cm. First let's arrange the numbers in ascending order:

14.6, 14.9, 14.9, 14.9, 15.0, 15.0, 15.0, 15.0, 15.1, 15.4

The mean is calculated like this:

$$\overline{X} = \frac{\sum\limits_{i=1}^{n} X_i}{n}$$

$$\overline{X} = \frac{14.6 + 14.9 + 14.9 + 14.9 + 15.0 + 15.0 + 15.0 + 15.0 + 15.1 + 15.4}{10}$$

$$\overline{X} = \frac{149.8}{10}$$

$$\overline{X} = 14.98$$

· ·

15.0 cm.

First let's arrange the numbers in ascending order:

14.6, 14.9, 14.9, 14.9, 15.0, 15.0, 15.0, 15.0, 15.1, 15.4

There is an even number, so the median is the average of the two middle values. The average of 15 and 15 is 15. So, the median is 15.0 cm.

· ·

15.0 cm.

First let's arrange the numbers in ascending order:

14.6, 14.9, 14.9, 14.9, 15.0, 15.0, 15.0, 15.0, 15.1, 15.4

To calculate the mode, list each value and its frequency in a table.

Length (cm)	Frequency
14.6	1
14.9	3
15.0	4
15.1	1
15.4	1

You see that 15.0 cm has the highest frequency, so the mode is 15.0 cm.

Do the candy bars meet length specifications for that hour?

. . . .

The graph describes the change in motion of a car.

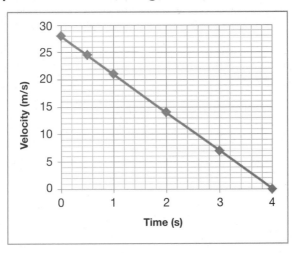

Which equation models the car's motion?
A. y = 7x + 28
B. y = 28x + 7
C. y = −28x + 7
D. y = −7x + 28

. . . .

Yes. All descriptors (mean, median, and mode) are in the range of 15.0 cm ± 0.5 cm, as are all the individual candy bars (14.6 cm to 15.4 cm). Therefore, the candy bars meet the specifications for that hour.

· ·

The correct answer is choice **D**. The graph shows that the velocity is decreasing linearly and can be described by the equation $y = -7x + 28$.

· ·

A man pushes a box horizontally across a **frictionless** surface for 15 m. He does 150 J of work. **How much net force did he apply to the box?**

A. 15 N

B. 10 N

C. 150 N

D. 1.0 N

. . . .

In a physics experiment, a student makes several measurements of the velocity of a sound wave from a tuning fork. The measurements (in m/s) are:

341, 343, 330, 335, 338, 345, 341

What is the mean of the sample data set?

. . . .

A molecular biologist wanted to make an artificial peptide containing three amino acids (there are 20 possible naturally occurring amino acids that he could use). Without repeating any amino acids, how many permutations are there?

A. 1,140

B. 6,840

C. 7,980

D. 3.2 million

The correct answer is choice **B**. Here's the solution:

Given: $W = 150$ J, $d = 15$ m

Unknown: $F_{net} = ?$

$W = F_{net}d$. Rearrange to find F_{net}:

$F_{net} = \dfrac{W}{d}$

$F_{net} = \dfrac{150\ J}{15\ m}$

$F_{net} = 10$ N

. . . .

339. Here's the solution:

$$\overline{X} = \dfrac{\sum\limits_{i=1}^{n} X_i}{n}$$

$\overline{X} = \dfrac{330 + 335 + 338 + 341 + 341 + 343 + 345}{7}$

$\overline{X} = \dfrac{2{,}373}{7}$

$\overline{X} = 339$

. . . .

The correct answer is choice **B**. Here's the solution:

$_nP_r = \dfrac{n!}{(n-r)!}$

$_{20}P_3 = \dfrac{20!}{(20-3)!}$

$_{20}P_3 = \dfrac{20!}{17!}$

$_{20}P_3 = \dfrac{20 \cdot 19 \cdot 18 \cdot \cancel{17 \cdot 16 \cdot 15 \cdot 14 \cdot 13 \cdot 12 \cdot 11 \cdot 10 \cdot 9 \cdot 8 \cdot 7 \cdot 6 \cdot 5 \cdot 4 \cdot 3 \cdot 2 \cdot 1}}{\cancel{17 \cdot 16 \cdot 15 \cdot 14 \cdot 13 \cdot 12 \cdot 11 \cdot 10 \cdot 9 \cdot 8 \cdot 7 \cdot 6 \cdot 5 \cdot 4 \cdot 3 \cdot 2 \cdot 1}}$

$_{20}P_3 = 20 \cdot 19 \cdot 18$

$_{20}P_3 = 6{,}840$

A student observes a chemical reaction in a series of tubes. After 5 minutes of reaction time, she rates the development of blue color on a scale of 1 to 5 (1 = pale blue, 5 = navy blue). The results are shown in the table.

Tube Number	Relative Color
A	3
B	5
C	1
D	4
E	2

Which represents the series of tubes in order from least color development to most color development?

A. A < B < C < D < E
B. C < E < A < D < B
C. E < D < A < B < C
D. E < D < C < B < A

. . . .

The correct answer is choice **B**. The tubes are in the correct order from least color development (Tube C = 1) to most color development (Tube B = 5).

A chemistry student conducts an investigation on the behavior of gases. He knows that pressure, volume, and temperature are variables and keeps the amount of gas constant. In three experiments, he keeps one variable fixed, while he varies another and measures the third. The results are plotted on graphs.

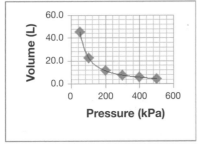

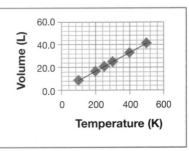

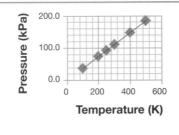

Which conclusions about gas behavior are true?
A. Temperature is inversely related to pressure and directly related to volume, while pressure is inversely related to volume.
B. Pressure is inversely related to both volume and temperature, while volume is directly related to temperature.
C. Volume is inversely related to pressure and directly related to temperature, while pressure is directly related to temperature.
D. The amount of gas is directly related to pressure and temperature, but inversely related to volume.

· ·

The correct answer is choice **C**. The first graph shows that volume is inversely related to pressure, the second graph shows that volume is directly related to temperature, and the third graph shows that pressure is directly related to temperature.

Which set of data accurately describes a car's motion under constant deceleration?

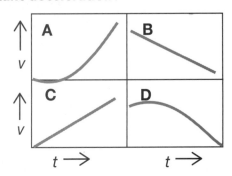

. . . .

A clinical researcher has learned that five slots have opened up in a clinical drug trial. Fifty applicants are eligible for the positions. Which is the possible number of permutations?
A. 250
B. 2,118,760
C. 254,251,200
D. 15,625,000,000

. . . .

A 2,000-kg truck accelerates at 40,000 m/s². What is the force acting on the truck?
A. 200 N
B. 40,000 N
C. 40 million N
D. 80 million N

The correct answer is **set B**. This data indicates the car is decelerating at a constant rate, the slope of the line.

· ·

The correct answer is choice **C**. Here's the solution.

$$_nP_r = \frac{n!}{(n-r)!}$$

$$_{50}P_5 = \frac{50!}{(50-5)!}$$

$$_{50}P_5 = \frac{50!}{45!}$$

$$_{50}P_5 = \frac{50 \cdot 49 \cdot 48 \cdot 47 \cdot 46 \cdot \cancel{45!}}{\cancel{45!}}$$

$$_{50}P_5 = 50 \cdot 49 \cdot 48 \cdot 47 \cdot 46$$

$$_{50}P_5 = 254{,}251{,}200$$

· ·

The correct answer is choice **D**. Here's the solution:

Given: $a = 40{,}000$ m/s^2, $m = 2{,}000$ kg

Unknown: $F_{net} = ?$

$a = \frac{F_{net}}{m}$. Rearrange to find F_{net}:

$F_{net} = ma$

$F_{net} = (2{,}000 \text{ kg})(40{,}000 \text{ m/s}^2)$

$F_{net} = 80{,}000{,}000$ N or 80 million N

A chemistry student conducts an experiment in which he keeps the temperature and volume of a gas constant. He increases the amount of the gas and measures the pressure. The data are shown in the table. He creates a graph in his lab report and the teacher marks it wrong.

Amount (mol)	P (kPa)
0	0
1	101
2	203
3	304
4	405
5	506

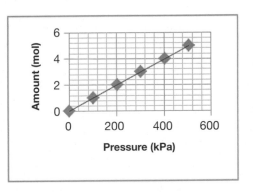

Which error did the student commit in making the graph?

A. The x-axis is not graded in even increments.
B. The y-axis is not graded in even increments.
C. There should be no line through the data points.
D. The variables are plotted on the wrong axes.

The correct answer is choice **D**. Amount is the independent variable and should be plotted on the x-axis. In contrast, pressure is the dependent variable and should be plotted on the y–axis.

Which of the graphs correctly depicts constant positive velocity?

A

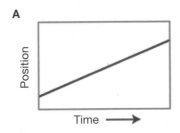

B

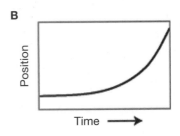

C

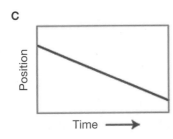

D

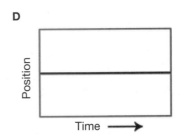

. . . .

Work is a force acting on an object to move it across a distance. Inclined planes make work easier by providing a smooth surface for objects to slide or roll across. Pushing a stroller up a ramp is easier than pushing it up a flight of stairs. When going down a ramp, the gravitational pull on the stroller may be all that the stroller needs to begin rolling and gain velocity.

The velocity of a moving object can be determined by the following formula:

$$\text{velocity} = \frac{\text{distance}}{\text{time}}$$

If a stroller travels with a forward velocity of four m/s for a time of two seconds, then the distance covered is _____ meters. (You may use a calculator to complete this question.)

. . . .

Graph A is the correct one. Velocity is speed with direction, and it is calculated by dividing the distance traveled by the time it took to cover that distance. On this graph, time is increasing to the right, and position is increasing constantly with time. At any point on graph A, the position divided by time will produce the same number, indicating constant positive velocity.

· ·

The correct answer is **eight** meters. The formula for velocity, $v = \frac{distance}{time}$, can be rearranged to solve for distance. In this case, $d = v \times t$, which is four m/s multiplied by two seconds.

· ·

Which of the following materials would be a good insulator?
A. a tile floor because it transfers heat away from skin
B. a steel spoon because it conducts heat from boiling liquids
C. a wool blanket because it slows the transfer of heat from skin
D. a copper pipe because it accelerates the transfer of heated materials

· ·

Every chemical reaction needs a certain amount of energy to get started, as illustrated in the graph.

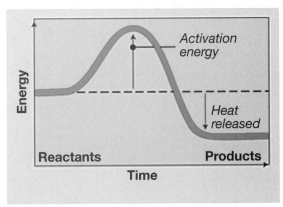

What type of reaction is shown?
A. endothermic, because energy is required after activation to continue the reaction
B. exothermic, because additional energy is needed in order to complete the reaction
C. exothermic, because the energy level of the products is lower than the energy level of the starting materials
D. endothermic, because the energy level of the final materials is higher than that of the starting materials

· ·

The correct answer is choice **C**. Materials such as wool are good insulators because they are poor conductors of heat. A wool blanket will slow the transfer of heat from the body so that it feels warmer.

. . . .

The correct answer is choice **C**. The graph shows that additional energy is not needed to complete the reaction; energy is given off as the reaction takes place. As a result, the energy level of the products is lower than the energy level of the starting materials.

. . . .

The amount of kinetic energy a moving object has depends on its velocity and mass. Kinetic energy can be calculated by using the following formula:

$$\text{kinetic energy} = \frac{\text{mass} \times \text{velocity}^2}{2}$$

Which of the following would have the most kinetic energy?
A. a truck driving 10 m/s
B. a bicycle traveling 10 m/s
C. a car stopped at a red light
D. a school bus parked on a hill

. . . .

Almost all the weight of a carbon atom comes from which of these particles?
A. protons only
B. neutrons and electrons
C. protons and neutrons
D. protons and electrons

. . . .

The correct answer is choice **A**. While a truck and a school bus may have similar mass, the school bus is parked, indicating a velocity of zero. Thus, the truck moving at any velocity will have the highest kinetic energy. Similarly, even though the bicycle is in motion, the greater mass of the truck will contribute to its larger kinetic energy.

· ·

The correct answer is choice **C**. Almost all the weight of an atom comes from the protons and neutrons in its nucleus. Neutrons weigh exactly one atomic mass unit, and protons weigh almost one atomic mass unit (1.67×10^{-24} grams).

· ·

Examine the diagram of an atom shown here.

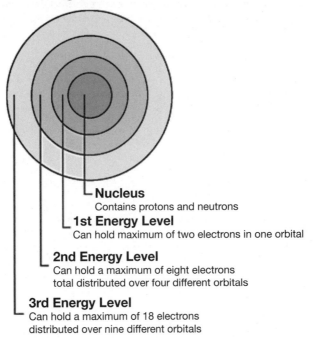

Nucleus
Contains protons and neutrons

1st Energy Level
Can hold maximum of two electrons in one orbital

2nd Energy Level
Can hold a maximum of eight electrons
total distributed over four different orbitals

3rd Energy Level
Can hold a maximum of 18 electrons
distributed over nine different orbitals

Which of these would be found in the first energy level?
A. eight neutrons
B. 18 electrons
C. protons and neutrons
D. no more than two electrons

The correct answer is choice **D**. The first energy level of an atom can hold a maximum of two electrons in one orbital. Each energy level is capable of holding a specific number of electrons.

A cleaning service wants to offer a natural alternative to the industrial products it normally uses. Instead of bleach, the company uses a mixture of vinegar and baking soda. When the liquid vinegar and powdered baking soda combine, a bubbly gas is produced. What chemical property is observed?

A. flammability
B. color change
C. volume
D. reactivity

. . . .

The correct answer is choice **D**, **reactivity**. Reactivity is the tendency of a substance to undergo a chemical reaction, either by itself or with other materials, and to release energy. Reactivity with other chemicals is evidenced when the baking soda and vinegar combine and react to create carbon dioxide gas, as seen by the bubbles.

The following chart lists the mechanical properties of different metals and alloys.

Toughness	Brittleness	Ductility	Malleability	Corrosion Resistance
Copper	White cast iron	Gold	Gold	Gold
Nickel	Gray cast iron	Silver	Silver	Platinum
Iron	Hardened steel	Platinum	Aluminum	Silver
Magnesium	Bismuth	Iron	Copper	Mercury
Zinc	Manganese	Nickel	Tin	Copper
Aluminum	Bronzes	Copper	Lead	Lead
Lead	Aluminum	Aluminum	Zinc	Tin
Tin	Brass	Tungsten	Iron	Nickel
Cobalt	Structural steels	Zinc		Iron
Bismuth	Zinc	Tin		Zinc
	Monel	Lead		Magnesium
	Tin			Aluminum
	Copper			
	Iron			

A jewelry designer wants to work with new types of materials. She needs a metal that is easy to shape, is not easily broken, and is resistant to tarnishing. Based on the chart, which material would be the best choice?

A. gold
B. nickel
C. bismuth
D. manganese

The correct answer is choice **A**, **gold**, because it tops the list for corrosion resistance and will not tarnish. It is also malleable, so it is easy to shape, but will not break easily because it is not brittle.

Hydrogen peroxide (H_2O_2) is stored in dark, opaque containers to slow the natural breakdown of the compound.

The reaction is summarized by this formula:

$$2\ H_2O_2 \rightarrow \underline{\hspace{1cm}} H_2O + O_2$$

Write the missing number of water molecules on the line.

· ·

In a chemical formula, subscripts show the ratio of one kind of atom to another. For example, NH_3 shows that there are three hydrogen atoms for every one nitrogen atom.

Examine the following ratios:
• twice as many sodium atoms as carbon atoms
• three times as many oxygen atoms as carbon atoms

Which chemical formula correctly shows the ratios described?

A. Na_2CO_3
B. $NaCO_3$
C. Na_3CO_2
D. Na_6CO_{12}

· ·

What is velocity?

$2 H_2O_2 \rightarrow \mathbf{2} H_2O + O_2$

The breakdown of hydrogen peroxide into water and oxygen is summarized as $2 H_2O_2 \rightarrow 2 H_2O + O_2$. The two balances the equation because there are two water molecules to equal four hydrogens.

· ·

The correct answer is choice **A, Na$_2$CO$_3$**. This formula shows sodium with a subscript of 2, indicating twice as many atoms as the one carbon atom. Oxygen has a subscript of 3, three times more than the single carbon atom.

· ·

The rate that a position changes in a constant direction per unit of time. Common units are meters per second (m/s).

What is the definition of volume?

. . . .

What is valence?

. . . .

What is a transverse wave?

A cubic measurement that measures how many cubic units it takes to fill a solid figure:

- Cube: $V = s^3$, where s is the length of any edge of the cube.
- Rectangular solid: $V = \text{length} \times \text{width} \times \text{height}$
- Square pyramid: $V = \frac{1}{3} \times (\text{base edge})^2 \times \text{height}$
- Cone: $V = \frac{1}{3} \times \pi \times \text{radius}^2 \times \text{height}$; π is approximately equal to 3.14.
- Cylinder: $V = \pi \times \text{radius}^2 \times \text{height}$; π is approximately equal to 3.14
- Prism: $V = B \times h$ (the area of the base $\times$ the height)

. . . .

The combining power of an element as shown by the number of electrons that are in the outer atomic shell and can participate in a chemical reaction.

. . . .

A wave in which the motion of the particles in the medium is perpendicular to the direction of wave propagation. Light is an example of a transverse wave.

What is the definition of tension?

. . . .

What is a spontaneous reaction?

. . . .

What is the speed of light?

The force that acts on and is transferred along ropes, strings, and chains.

· ·

A reaction that does not require an external source of energy to proceed.

· ·

The speed of light in a vacuum (186,282 miles per second) is the fastest speed possible. As light travels in other materials, it will change speed. The speed of light in any material is still the fastest speed possible in that material. Commonly denoted by the symbol c.

What is a series circuit?

· ·

What is a reversible reaction?

· ·

A circuit with only one path for an electrical current to follow. The current in each element in a series circuit is the same.

· ·

A reaction in which products can revert back into reactants.

· ·

Refer to the following passage to answer the next four questions.

A student is conducting an experiment involving inertia with a dozen eggs, one of which is hard-boiled. Inertia is defined as the property of matter by which it resists any change in velocity. The student spins each egg and then touches it to stop the egg from moving. The student observes that the hard-boiled egg spins and stops easily as it is touched, but the raw eggs continue moving even after being touched to stop the spin.

Why does the hard-boiled egg stop spinning so easily?

. . . .

Why do the raw eggs continue trying to move?

. . . .

How does this experiment reference inertia?

The mass inside the egg is solid and evenly distributed.

· ·

The liquid portion inside the egg causes a drag effect that resists the spin initially and then resists being made motionless at the end.

· ·

Since inertia is defined by resistance to change in velocity, it can be determined that a raw egg has a greater tendency toward inertia due to its liquid portion than a hard-boiled egg.

What variable of this experiment has not been fully determined?

. . . .

The surface on which the eggs are spun. In order to determine that the surface is not contributing to inertia on either the hard-boiled egg or the raw eggs, the surface should be smooth and frictionless.

· ·

NOTES

NOTES